The Problem of the Obelisks, From a Study of the Unfinished Obelisk at Aswan

The Problem of the Obelisks

FIG. 1.—OBELISKS OF TUTHMÔSIS I (*left*) AND HATSHEPSOWET (*right*) AT KARNAK.
(*The nearer obelisk leans to the left owing to soil-subsidence.*)

[*Frontispiece.*

THE PROBLEM OF THE OBELISKS

FROM A STUDY OF THE UNFINISHED OBELISK AT ASWAN

BY

R. ENGELBACH
Assoc. C. & G. Inst.

(Chief Inspector of Antiquities, Upper Egypt (Author of RIQQEH, 1915; THE ASWAN OBELISK, 1922; HARAGEH, 1923, *etc.)*

ILLUSTRATED

T. FISHER UNWIN, LIMITED
LONDON ADELPHI TERRACE

First published in 1923

PREFACE

THIS book has been written, not only to give the general reader the results of the latest researches on the ages-old problem as to how the obelisks were extracted and erected

THE PROBLEM OF THE OBELISKS
R. ENGELBACH

ERRATA

Page 19, last line, for "Ramôse" read "Seti I."
,, 48, lines 13, 20, and 22, for "3·15 inches" read "·315 inch."
,, 60, line 5, for "rollers" read "baulks."
,, 70, lines 15 and 17, for $\frac{1}{1000}$ read $\frac{1}{100}$.

quarry in 1921 and 1922 have already been published by the Antiquities Department, under the title of *The Aswan Obelisk, with some remarks on the Ancient Engineering*, of which this is practically a popular edition. It has been entirely re-written and re-arranged, omitting the rather elaborate calculations on stresses and leverages which are given at length in the official volume, but giving in far greater detail

PREFACE

THIS book has been written, not only to give the general reader the results of the latest researches on the ages-old problem as to how the obelisks were extracted and erected in ancient times, but also to furnish visitors to Aswan with a full description of the huge unfinished obelisk lying in the quarries a short distance from the Cataract Hotel, which has thrown a great deal of light on the ancient methods. I have included in it, for comparison, brief accounts of the removal and re-erection in modern times of the Vatican, Paris, London and New York obelisks. No detailed account of the Aswan Obelisk has yet appeared in any guide-book.

The results of my clearance of the obelisk quarry in 1921 and 1922 have already been published by the Antiquities Department, under the title of *The Aswan Obelisk, with some remarks on the Ancient Engineering,* of which this is practically a popular edition. It has been entirely re-written and re-arranged, omitting the rather elaborate calculations on stresses and leverages which are given at length in the official volume, but giving in far greater detail the results of my experiments with the scale model shown in figs. 27–33, which Mr. Donaldson, of the Egyptian State Railways, kindly made to my design. No photographs of this model have been hitherto published.

Although more than a year has elapsed since sending the manuscript of *The Aswan Obelisk* to press, I have not had to modify my views on the ancient methods in any point of importance; further study of the quarry has, however, induced me to omit the alternative suggestion on the manner in which the obelisk was rolled clear of the quarry (page 53) and to assert, with some confidence, that sleds were an essential in the transport of all large obelisks.

To the reader who may charge me with expending so much space on such a restricted subject as that of the making of obelisks, I would recall the deathbed answer of the old professor to his friends, who had asked him if he did not think he had wasted his life by devoting it exclusively to the study of Greek prepositions. He replied: "It is true; I should have confined myself to those governing the Dative!" Like him, I feel that I have unduly digressed in Chapter VIII, when so much remains to be discussed on the mechanical side.

In explaining the various processes, I have tried to indicate clearly where fact ends and deduction begins, and frankly to admit—as in the case of the details of the transport barges—where there is not sufficient evidence on which to speculate, or when any stage of the mechanical history of the obelisk is not clear to me.

There is an increasing demand, among the 10,000 visitors who come to Egypt each year, for facts about the arts, crafts, engineering and practical life of the Egyptians; in other words, for a compact account of what is known on a subject that interests them; and there is a corresponding and natural dislike to descriptions of the never-ending scenes of gods and kings, which, after all, convey very little information even to the archæologist. There is a surprising difference between the taste of the average visitor now and that of fifteen years ago. Then the chief point of remark about the tourist was his Baedeker and his boredom; now Breasted's *Ancient Records* and the latest archæological works are constantly seen in his hands, in addition to that excellent guide-book.

In the following pages I have been occasionally guilty of levity. My defence is that it is as a sort of protest against a habit—so dear to the dilettanti in Egyptian lore—of never speaking of anything "Ancient Egyptian" except in sepulchral tones and with bated breath, lest a *curse* fall upon them! As a matter of fact the Egyptian, apart from his religion, was essentially a practical man, and by no means opposed to a little levity; one has only to read the text accompanying some of the banqueting scenes in the tombs—such as that of Paheri at El-Kâb—to be convinced of this. Further, this book deals with *work*, and lacks the "romance" popularly associated with the gods, graves and ghosts of ancient Egypt. I have only dipped into the graveyard for purely secular information, such as the careers of the ancient architects. My feeble attempts to brighten up a rather "tough" subject may therefore be pardoned, if not approved.

On the subject of the transcription of Egyptian names, a word of explanation may not be out of place. I am constantly asked, "Which should it be: Tuthmôsis, Thothmes, Tahutimes, Dhutmose, Tuthmose or Thutmosis?" or: "Was the Queen called Hatshepsut, Hatshepsôwet, Hatshepsuit, Hatshopsitou or Hatasoo?" The reason for these variants is that the Egyptians wrote their names in consonants only, except—apparently under protest—when they indicated the *presence* of an initial vowel or final *i*. The system adopted here is practically that given by Dr. Alan Gardiner in his *Topographical Catalogue of the Private Tombs of Thebes*, and that is an attempt to reconstruct the names, following the latest researches in the ancient vocalisation. In the case of kings, where the Greek or Manethonian form is well known and appears to be close to the probable articulation, it has been retained. Thus we say Hatshepsôwet, Dhuthotpe and Sennemût, but Tuthmôsis, Amenophis and Ramesses. This system is being adopted by the Survey of Egypt for their future publications. The variants given in Appendix II will, I hope, clear up all the reader's difficulties in this respect.

In collecting the history of the obelisks and their architects for Chapter VIII, I am greatly indebted to Prof. J. H. Breasted's invaluable *Ancient Records*, which give, in a handy form, translations of every historical document in Egypt. Though in most cases the translations given in that chapter are based on Prof. Breasted's work, I have occasionally sacrificed his strictly literal translation in order to give the reader a freer rendering.

My thanks are due to the Antiquities Department of the Egyptian Government for permission to reproduce from *The Aswan Obelisk* figures 5–11, 13–20, 22, 25, 26, 34–36; to Messrs. Macmillan and Co. for the loan of the blocks for figures 21, 23 and 24; and to Messrs. Harmsworths, Ltd., for permission to reproduce the photographs on figures 1, 2 and 38–40 from my article on obelisks in *Wonders of the Past.* Photos 3, 4 and 18 were taken by Mr. A. M. MacGillivray, of Aswan; 1, 2, 38–40 by Gaddis and Seif, Luxor; the remainder are mine.

PREFACE

CONTENTS

LIST OF ILLUSTRATIONS

THE PROBLEM OF THE OBELISKS

CHAPTER I

OBELISKS AND QUARRIES

OBELISKS have always held a great attraction for visitors to Egypt throughout the ages. From the time of Assurbanipal II onwards nearly every foreign controller of Egypt has removed one or more as a souvenir. Though there must have been several score of large obelisks in the country—Karnak alone had at least thirteen—there now remain but five standing. Earthquakes, soil-subsidence and the foreigner have indeed taken a toll.

Though records of obelisks extend back into the Old Kingdom, and fragments of them have been discovered, the earliest complete example is that of King Senusret I of the XIIth dynasty at El-Mataria, near Cairo, shown in fig. 2. The others are those of Tuthmôsis I, Queen Hatshepsôwet and Seti II at Karnak, and the obelisk in front of Luxor temple dating to the reign of Ramesses II. Of these, that of Tuthmôsis I (frontispiece) is in a rather dangerous condition owing to the settling of its pedestal, and that of

Seti II is only a miniature obelisk of gritstone, of which there must have been hundreds in the country. Against this Rome has nine over 20 feet high, while Constantinople, Paris, London and New York all have one large obelisk, not to mention several small ones in museums, private collections and gardens.

In ancient times there must have been a great number of large obelisks in Egypt. Seti I tells us that he "filled Heliopolis with obelisks," and Ramesses II is known to have had fourteen in Tanis alone, though whether he erected them or merely usurped them, according to his habit, is uncertain. Besides the temples of the great centres such as Karnak and Luxor, Heliopolis and Tanis, many of the temples in other places must have had them. We have actual records of obelisks at Philæ, Elephantine, Soleb (in Nubia), the mortuary temple of Amenophis III behind the Colossi of Thebes, and elsewhere. The total number of obelisks exceeding 30 feet in length must have been well over fifty.

The origin and religious significance of the obelisk are somewhat obscure. In the royal sanctuaries of the fifth dynasty kings on the margin of the western desert at Abusir, not far from the Pyramids of Gizeh, the obelisk took the place of the holy of holies of the later temples. Recent excavations have shown that these obelisks were very different from those now familiar to visitors, as the length of the base was fully one-third that of the shaft, which was of masonry and merely served the

FIG. 2.—OBELISK OF SENUSRET I AT MATARIA, NEAR CAIRO.
(*Pages 17, 30 and 111.*)

purpose of elevating the sacred pyramid or *benben(t)*, as the Egyptians called it—the real emblem of the sun. The obelisks of Upper Egypt, on the other hand, had no very definite connection with sun-worship, their only function being an additional decoration to the pylons, though it is known that they were greatly venerated and offerings were made to them. They were erected in pairs, and when Tuthmôsis III (p. 109) put up a single one at Karnak, he says that it was the first time that this had been done. Until we know how early obelisks were placed before the pylons of Upper Egypt, it is rather difficult to say whether they were developed from the fifth dynasty sun-obelisks or independently, particularly when one realises that, if a high, thin stone monument is desired, the obelisk is the only practical form which is pleasing to the eye and convenient for inscribing. In any case, the subject is really outside the scope of this book, which deals rather with the mechanical side of obelisk-lore. A discussion of the obelisk as a sun-emblem pure and simple is given in Prof. J. H. Breasted's *Development of Religion and Thought in Ancient Egypt* (Hodder and Stoughton) on pages 11, 15 and 71.

The artistic taste of the ancient Egyptian differed considerably from ours and, to our minds, he was in the habit of decorating objects which do not need any decoration whatever. He had—like the modern Egyptian—a perfect mania for painting and gilding everything. In the tomb of Ramôse at Thebes (No. 55) he has painted in gaudy colours the most wonderfully detailed reliefs, and we know for certain that he overlaid the huge fir-trees, which formed the pylon flagstaves, with bands and tips of electrum or copper. Obelisks did not escape this craze, and as far back as our records go they were capped with electrum, copper or gold. The Arab historian ‘Abd El-Latîf, writing as late as 1201 A.D., states that the *two* Heliopolis (Mataria) obelisks still retained their copper caps, and that around them were other obelisks large and small, too numerous to mention (see page 111). Now only one remains.

The unfinished obelisk of Aswan, though its existence has been known for centuries, was never cleared until the end of the winter of 1922, when my Department granted me L.E. 75 to do so. In this work I was assisted by Mahmûd Eff. Mohammad and Mustafa Eff. Hasan of the Antiquities Department, who supervised the workmen.

Before the clearance, all the visitor could see of the obelisk was the top surface of the pyramidion and about 20 yards of shaft, which sloped down into a vast heap of sand, chips and granite boulders. It has now become one of the most visited sights in Aswan, since nothing of its kind is to be seen elsewhere.

Most persons, having seen the temples and tombs of Egypt, become more or less blasé to them. This is largely due to the fact that no-one—least of all the dragomans—brings home to them the enormous difficulties the Egyptians overcame. They dismiss them as beyond their understanding, and many closer students of the monuments than the average visitor have boldly affirmed that the Egyptians knew engines and forces of nature of which we are to-day ignorant. This is quite a wrong idea ; it is, as a matter of fact, far easier to explain every step in the mechanics of a large obelisk to the non-technical reader than those of an iron bridge. Though modern research robs the Egyptians of the magical powers attributed to them, it makes them more admirable in the eyes of the practical man, as it shows that they could do, with the most primitive tools, feats of engineering which we, with some 3,000 years of mechanical progress behind us, are barely able to copy.

A study of the Aswan Obelisk enables the visitor to look with different eyes on the finished monuments, and to realise, not only the immense labour expended in transporting the giant blocks and the years of tedious extraction of stone in the quarries, but the heartbreaking failures which must sometimes have driven the old engineers to the verge of despair before a perfect monument could be presented by the king to his god. Nowadays, if anything gets out of position, a jack, a winch or a crane is called for, and the trouble is soon put right ; in ancient times a colossus or an obelisk which came down badly on to its pedestal was something in the nature of a tragedy. A perfect monument teaches us little of their engineering ; an imperfect or unfinished piece of work may teach us much. Thus the obelisk of Hatshepsôwet at Karnak, standing askew on its pedestal, which must have been a perpetual sore point to Sennemût, its engineer, is useful to us, as it enables us at once to rule out the levering-up theories put forward by Gorringe and others who have written on the subject (page 67).

The Aswan Obelisk is a piece of work that failed, not through any fault of the workers, but owing to an unexpected fissure in the rock. It must have been galling beyond words to the Egyptians to abandon it after all the time and trouble they had expended, but to-day we are grateful for their failure, as it teaches us more about their methods than any other monument in Egypt.

The great quarries of Aswan and Silsileh are quite untouched as regards excavation, which is one of the reasons why our knowledge on the extraction of stone is so very unsatisfactory. In spite of this there is quite a considerable literature on the subject, mostly done either by engineers (on a brief visit) with no knowledge of archæology to enable them to control their assertions, or by archæologists to whom engineering is a sealed mystery. While the publication of a new grammatical form or historical point will evoke a perfect frenzy of contradiction in the little world of Egyptology, the most absurd statements on a mechanical problem will be left unquestioned, and, what is worse, accepted. In most branches of modern archæology the alleged savant must work in conjunction with the specialist, and the specialist needed for the subject under discussion is the foreman quarryman. This was brought home to me with great force when I was at work on the obelisk, and I shall never forget the ease nor the contempt with which an old Italian quarryman disproved some of my then most cherished theories. His range of knowledge may have been limited, but it was painfully accurate.

A walk round the quarries between the railway and the Reservoir road at Aswan well repays the trouble. Here we may see gigantic embankments, some nearly half a mile in length, on which the great blocks were transported from the high desert down to the Nile; we can see half-finished sarcophagi (fig. 9, page 42) and statues, abandoned no one knows why, in various stages of completion; we can see inscriptions, some readable and some not, painted or cut on the boulders by the ancient engineers, and everywhere we may see the marks of their wedges, some showing where a block has been removed, others where the wedge has failed to act, or has split the rock in the wrong direction. The site clamours for excavation, which might well reveal chippings from the chisels used in cutting the granite, and thus settle, once and for all, whether they were of highly tempered copper or not; another abandoned monument might give us conclusive information as to the methods by which they were detached from below, and how it was intended to roll them out from their beds. Excavation might well furnish us with ancient levers and rollers—or traces of them—which are hardly known at present, and then only of small size. A big quarry has never been cleared, and we cannot believe that the small area excavated round the obelisk has revealed all the secrets. The explanation of the neglect of the quarries is that they are not likely to afford good museum-pieces.

With an expenditure of L.E. 500 a really comprehensive study of quarrying could be made, which would surely add greatly to our present knowledge.

CHAPTER II

DESCRIPTION OF THE ASWAN OBELISK

THE obelisk lies in a quarry on the south-east side of the mediæval Arab cemetery, being about a quarter of an hour's drive from the Cataract Hotel. The best time for visiting it is either early in the morning or just before sunset, as it is at these times that the guide-lines on the upper surface of the obelisk and the curious structure of the trench surrounding it are most clearly visible.

The best general view is obtained by passing over the new retaining wall at the butt, and thence up past the vertical face of rock to the hill above it. Even from there, owing to fore-shortening, it is difficult to realise the enormous size of the monument, which is one-third as high again as the largest obelisk in Karnak, and more than triple the weight.

Its complete dimensions are as follows :—

Length	137 feet.
Base	13 feet 9 inches.
Pyramidion base	8 feet 2 inches.
Pyramidion height	14 feet 9 inches.
Weight (if it had been extracted) ..	1,168 tons.

Photographs of the obelisk from the tip and butt are given in figs. 3 and 4, and a plan of the quarry, with sections, in fig. 7, p. 38. From the latter it will be seen that the impression gained from the ground, that the obelisk is abnormally thick for its length, is incorrect.

It is fortunate that, in this small quarry, we can see so many different examples of the methods of the old workmen. At B, fig. 22 (shown close in fig. 8), we see examples of the action of ancient wedges and chisels, showing how easily the Egyptians could cut granite. It appears that all this wedging was with the object of removing the rock to let the tip of the obelisk pass when it was rolled out of the quarry. At A and C, fig. 7, p. 38, we can see modern chisel-dressing and what is probably a more recent method of using the wedge, which is by cutting a long channel instead of a series of small slots. Granite, rotted by the action of fire, can be picked up almost anywhere in the quarry; test-shafts, sunk early in the work to study the quality of the granite, can be seen at C and D in fig. 7, and the first can even now be traced up to the original surface of the quarry. The trench, by means of which it was intended to separate the obelisk from the rock, is another and unique example of the ancient method of quarrying, and is discussed in Chapter IV. The vertical face of rock above the obelisk is nothing but the interior wall of another perimeter-trench, from before which a monument—possibly an obelisk—has been removed (fig. 18, p. 50). On this face we have the records of the work of the various shifts employed (fig. 13, p. 44 and p. 46). Neither this nor the obelisk-trench show how the monuments were to be detached from below,

FIG. 3.—ASWAN OBELISK FROM THE EAST.
(*Page* 25.)

FIG. 4. ASWAN OBELISK FROM THE WEST.
(*Page* 25.)

the one since a sufficient depth had not been reached, the other because the bed has been removed; but so that nothing may be lacking, above the quarry-face there still remains the bed from which a monument of about 23 feet long has been taken. We could wish for a larger monument from which we might study the under-cutting, since what applies to a medium-sized block does not always apply to those of very large size; but we must be grateful for what we have.

As to the date of the obelisk, there is very little indication of it; since it was a failure, it was in nobody's interest to record it. It may have been of the time of Queen Hatshepsôwet (i.e., about 1500 B.C.), since large obelisks seem to have been the rule in her time. Further, the outline of a smaller obelisk drawn upon the surface of the large one (figs. 6 and 7), which can be well seen just after sunrise, is of almost exactly the same dimensions as that now known as the Lateran obelisk at Rome, the work of Tuthmôsis III, her co-regent and successor. These evidences of date should, however, be accepted with a good deal of caution.

The obelisk was abandoned owing to fissures in the granite, as the possibility of erecting a very large obelisk depends entirely on the rock being sound, particularly near the middle (p. 75). Here, although the granite is of extremely good quality, it is by no means flawless, and from the very outset of the work the cracks and fissures seem to have given the ancient engineers a great deal of anxiety. Though parting fairly evenly under the action of wedges, the natural fissures in the granite are most erratic ; a small fissure in one level or position may, in a couple of metres, become a gaping crack into which one could insert the blade of a knife ; conversely, what appears to be a deep fissure may disappear at a lower level. Hence each crack had to be rigorously examined to see its probable effect on the completed obelisk. The methods by which this examination is carried out are described on page 37.

Fig. 7 (p. 38) is a plan, with sections, of the obelisk, and shows all the fissures (lettered *a*, *b*, *c*, &c.), and nearly all the guide-lines (indicated by Greek letters). These show clearly that attempt after attempt was made, by reducing the size of the proposed obelisk, to obtain one in which the granite was free from flaws.

For those who wish to examine the history of these attempts in greater detail the following notes may be of service. Very early in the work—almost after the roughing-out was finished—it was found that fissure *o*, which cuts off the corner of the obelisk, necessitated reducing its length from the butt end. It was therefore reduced 4 cubits, or 6 feet 10 inches, and a black line (π) drawn across the top surface of the obelisk and down the sides to mark off the reduction. The depth at which the trench was abandoned at the butt shows how early it was realised that a length of 137 feet was impossible. Almost as soon as this had been done it was

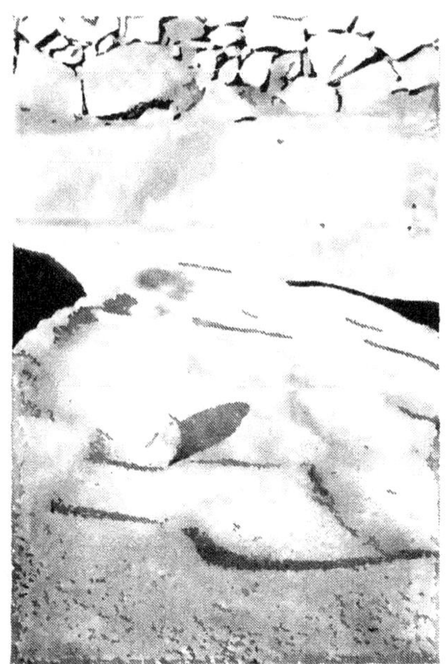

FIG. 5.—HAMMER-DRESSING ON PYRAMIDION OF ASWAN OBELISK.
(*Page 36.*)

FIG. 6.—OUTLINE OF SCHEME FOR REDUCING SIZE OF ASWAN OBELISK.
(*Pages 27 and 29.*)

found that fissures *a*, *b*, and *c* necessitated shortening the obelisk from this end also. The lines ι κ λ are the successive proposals for reducing the length of the shaft in order to obtain a flawless piece. Fissure *c*, however, showed clearly that the pyramidion must be kept quite clear of it, since it widens as it goes deeper. Fissures *j*, *k*, *l* and *m* would have made the quarry (or south) side of the obelisk liable to split, so in a last attempt to obtain a perfect piece of stone the centre line η was shifted to θ, and a very much smaller obelisk set out from it. This, as has been noted before, is almost exactly the size of the Lateran obelisk. Even this scheme did not escape the fissures, since at *p* there is a large one, running right into the obelisk, which would make it unsound at its most vulnerable point, the centre. I have no doubt that the obelisk was abandoned owing to fissure *p*.

It may be of interest to the reader to compare the sizes and weights of some of the best-known obelisks. Those marked with an asterisk are scaled off photographs, making slight allowances for foreshortening. (See p. 30.)

It is perhaps no more than a coincidence that the outline for the Aswan "last attempt" has a base of exactly the same size as that of the fragment before Pylon VII at Karnak, namely, 10·3 feet, from which M. G. Legrain, the late Director of Works, deduced a height of 124 feet (37·77 metres). He assumed that the taper would be the same as that of Queen Hatshepsôwet's obelisk at Karnak, which, as a matter of fact, is less than all others, thus making the height greater than it would be with the average taper. Last year a fragment of the companion obelisk was found, from which it can be estimated accurately that the base of the pyramidion was 2·08 metres or 6·8 feet, which is very close to the Aswan outline.

OBELISK.	BASE (feet).	PYRAMIDION BASE (feet).	PYRAMIDION HEIGHT (feet).	TOTAL HEIGHT (feet).	TAPER (see footnote 2).	WEIGHT IN TONS.
Aswan	13·8	8·2	14·8	137	24·3	1,168
Aswan (later project)	10·3	6·6	17·4	105	23·7	507
Lateran[1]	9·8	6·2*	14·8*	105·6	29·3	455
Hatshepsôwet ..	7·9	5·8	9·7	97	42·8	323
Vatican	8·8	5·9	4·4	83	26·9	331
Luxor	8·2	5·1*	6·4*	82*	28·2	254
Paris	8·0	5·1	6·4	74	26·5	227
New York[1].. ..	7·7	5·3*	5·4*	69·6	29·0	193
London[1]	7·8	5·3*	5·4*	68·5	27·4	187
Mataria[1]	6·2	4·0*	6·6*	67	27·5	121
Tuthmôsis I ..	7·0	4·6	7·8	64	24·2	143

[1] After Gorringe, *Egyptian Obelisks.*

[2] By taper I mean the length of the shaft in which one unit decrease in width is observed.

All over the quarries at Aswan, and especially round the obelisk, may be seen hundreds of balls—some whole and some broken—of a very tough greenish-black stone known as *dolerite,* which occur naturally in some of the valleys in the eastern desert. It is a curious but incontestable fact that not only were the faces of monuments dressed by means of these balls—which has been long known—but that they were used for " cutting " out large monuments from the rock. In other words, they are the tools of the quarrymen.

On the face of the high rock C (in fig. 22, p. 60), nearest the obelisk, are two inscriptions, and traces of others now barely legible. One reads, in the Greek character:—

ΑΜ . . . . .
CΑΒΙΝΙΑΝΟC
CΕΡΑΠΕΙΩΝ
ΟΡCΟΥ

"Am . . . Sabinianos (and) Serapeiôn (sons) of Ursus." These are Greek forms of Latin names, probably those of early visitors to this quarry. Close to this inscription there is another name ΕΡΜΕΙΝΟC, Ermeinos, cut into the face of the rock.

Two large embankments, dating from ancient times, may be seen close to the quarry; one leads westwards from the quarry above the obelisk, and another of gigantic size leads from the low desert about 200 yards east of the obelisk up to the quarries on the high desert. This can be seen even from the Grenfell Tombs across the river. Neither of these embankments appears to have any connection with the great obelisk.

CHAPTER III

SETTING OUT AN OBELISK

IN the following chapters we will endeavour, by deduction from the facts observed, and from ancient records, to ascertain every step in the history of an obelisk from the moment when the ancient engineers arrived at Aswan, from whence all the obelisks come, to the moment when it is standing upright before the pylon in the temple.

Where the evidence is insufficient, as in the case of the details of the huge transport boats, we will merely record the meagre facts which have come down to us, as it would be unwise to credit the Egyptians, in order to explain a difficult point, with appliances or any knowledge which we are not certain that they possessed.

At Aswan the surface of the granite consists of huge boulders, some quite large enough to provide a door-jamb or even a shrine, but none which could possibly furnish a moderate-sized obelisk. It must have required great experience to judge whether there was likely to be a long, flawless piece at a moderate depth. Whether test-shafts were sunk to examine the quality of the granite in all deep work I do not know, but I think it most probable, though in my superficial survey of the quarries I have not found any examples besides the two in the obelisk quarry (fig. 7, at C and D).

The quickest and most economical way of removing the top layers of the stratum is by burning fires against the rock, which causes it to break up very easily, especially if water is poured on it while it is still hot—a method used in India at the present day. There is a good deal of evidence to show that the Egyptians used this method, and it seems that the fires must have been of papyrus reeds, which at that time probably grew abundantly here just as it infests certain parts of the upper reaches of the Nile now. There are indications that these fires were banked with bricks against the surface to be destroyed. Traces of burning are seen at A and B (fig. 18, p. 50), and burnt granite can be picked up almost anywhere. It may be remarked here that the burnt granite must be distinguished from the weathered granite and that decomposed by the ferruginous layers in the stratum, which are likely to be confused with it.

In the actual obelisk quarry, wedge-marks are seen only at one place. The large blocks removed by a series of wedges acting in a channel instead of in slots are almost certainly of a later date than that of the obelisk. The (now) entrance to the trench is also a later piece of work, as the fine chisel-dressing is of the modern type, and I even obtained a block from here which had a hole "jumped" for blasting with gunpowder. Although so few wedge-marks have been found in the work on the obelisk, I believe that they were freely used when necessary; where a large block could fall away from the parent rock, wedges were probably more quick than burning. They can be seen in thousands all over the quarries. They are usually driven from the top downwards, but some may be seen which have acted horizontally and some even from below. It has been asserted that the wedges themselves were of wood and made to expand by wetting them. Without wishing to deny that the Egyptians knew and used this method, I will merely observe that the taper of the slots seems so great, and the sides of the slots so smooth, that there would be a great tendency for the wedges to jump out after wetting rather than exert their pressure; another point is that it would be a somewhat difficult matter to wet a horizontal wedge, and still more difficult to do so from below. I am inclined to think that the normal method was to use metal—perhaps iron—wedges, with thin metal plates between the wedge and the stone which are now known as "feathers." The hammers may well have been of stone after the fashion of the Old Kingdom hammer from Gizeh (of black granite), shown in fig. 10, p. 42. The method used nowadays is to make, with a steel chisel, a series of small holes along the line where fracture is required, and by inserting small, fat, steel punches in them and giving them in turn, up and down the line, moderately hard blows with a sledge-hammer. In the clearance of the obelisk some hundreds of large blocks had to be broken up by this means before we could conveniently remove them. These had apparently been thrown down from the quarry above. Ancient iron wedges, perhaps dating to 800 B.C., are given in Petrie, *Tools and Weapons*, Plate XIII, B 16, 17. Some enormous wedge-slots may be seen at the top of the rock in fig. 8, which may well have been cut for use with expanding wooden wedges.

Having reduced the granite until they were satisfied that it was suitable for extracting an obelisk, and before dressing the surface in any way, they began to sink squarish holes round what was to be the perimeter or outline of the obelisk. This may well have been measured out by cords stretched over the rough surface. The traces of these pits can be best seen in the further trench in fig. 7, p. 38, no. 3. The method of making these pits is discussed in the next chapter. There are plenty of indications that they were begun before the surface of what was to be the obelisk had been made smooth. For reasons which will appear later, the work on the pits progressed a good deal more slowly than that on the trench, so that, by the time the work had reached the stage at which it was abandoned, the trench workers had almost caught up with those engaged on the pits. Their object appears to have been to obtain as much knowledge of the state of the granite below as possible, especially as regards any horizontal fissures which might be met with, unsuspected from above.

The next step, an extremely laborious process, was to render the surface flat. This was done entirely by bruising with the balls of dolerite which have been found in such profusion in the quarry. Examples of unfinished top-dressing can be seen at the pyramidion and near the butt, where the work was abandoned early (fig. 5, p. 28). Whether these balls were used by hand, or shod in some way on rammers, is doubtful. It seems likely that they were so mounted and worked by several men, as such blows were dealt that the balls were sometimes split in two—almost an impossibility by hand.

A smooth straight surface along and across what was to be the upper face of the obelisk was almost certainly obtained by the use of what we now call "boning-rods." These are a set of pieces of wood of exactly equal length, now usually made T-shaped. One rod is held upright at each end of the surface it is required to straighten. A man standing at one end can, if he sight along the top of these rods, see if a third rod, placed somewhere between them, is in a line with them or not. Thus the surface can be tested anywhere along the obelisk and corrected until it is quite flat. Boning-rods of small size, used for dressing moderately large blocks, have actually been found, and are published in Petrie, *Tools and Weapons*, Plate XLIX, B 44–46. These measure only about 3 inches high, and their tops were connected by a string. In the case of such a monument as an obelisk the string would sag and produce a concave error. The visual method, quite as simple and obvious, seems a legitimate assumption.

The accuracy in the work of obelisks is not of a very high order, unlike the tremendous accuracy seen in the Pyramids of Gizeh and certain Old and Middle Kingdom monuments. An error in the sides of the base is quite usual, sometimes amounting to several inches. The two obelisks which stood before the temple of Luxor were even different in height (see dimensions of Luxor and Paris obelisks on p. 30). It is well worth while to examine the faces of the Karnak and Mataria obelisks at the moment when they receive the sun's rays; it is then that one can see how considerable are the errors in flatness. In the former obelisk faint traces of the hammer-dressing, such as is seen in fig. 5, can be observed.

In the Luxor obelisk which was removed to Paris there appears to have been a convexity, intentionally left on the front face, to counteract the effect of concavity which is noticed in some high monuments. This was the regular practice in the case of Greek pillars, and is known as "entasis." I have not been able to trace it in any of the Karnak obelisks nor in the unfinished obelisk at Aswan.

As soon as a crack, fissure or even unusual discoloration appeared in any part of the obelisk, it had to be carefully examined to see how far it went, and whether it became wider as the work deepened. Three methods of examination are to be seen on the obelisk. The normal method was to hammer out a depression with the ubiquitous dolerite balls at what seemed to be the end of the fissure, leaving a small oblong fillet so as to compare the appearance of the granite at the surface with that at the bottom of the depression. These examinations can be seen in fig. 7 at *j*, *k*, *n* and *p*, *n* being also shown in fig. 4, p. 26. Another method of testing fissures is found at the base of the pyramidion; this consists of cutting, with a metal tool, an oblong hole, tapering sharply downwards, over the fissure. Here it was done to see the extent of fissures *b* and *d*. It is possible that this method was used when it was desired to save time, perhaps on the occasion of an inspection. The third method was to cut—and apparently polish—a deep narrow channel right along the fissure or discoloration. These channels are seen in fig. 7 at *g* and *h*, and in fig. 6, p. 28. It has been asserted that these channels are later attempts to cut up the obelisk for monumental stone, but this is not the case, as *g* is clearly a continuation of fissure *b*, and *h* could never have been used for detaching a piece from the parent rock. If one follows *i* down the north face of the obelisk three red lines can be seen which were drawn by the foreman for the guidance of the stonecutter.

It is rather difficult to say whether there is a difference of date between the examinations by channels and the others; it depends on the relative dates of the large obelisk and the last attempt. I do not think that there is any great

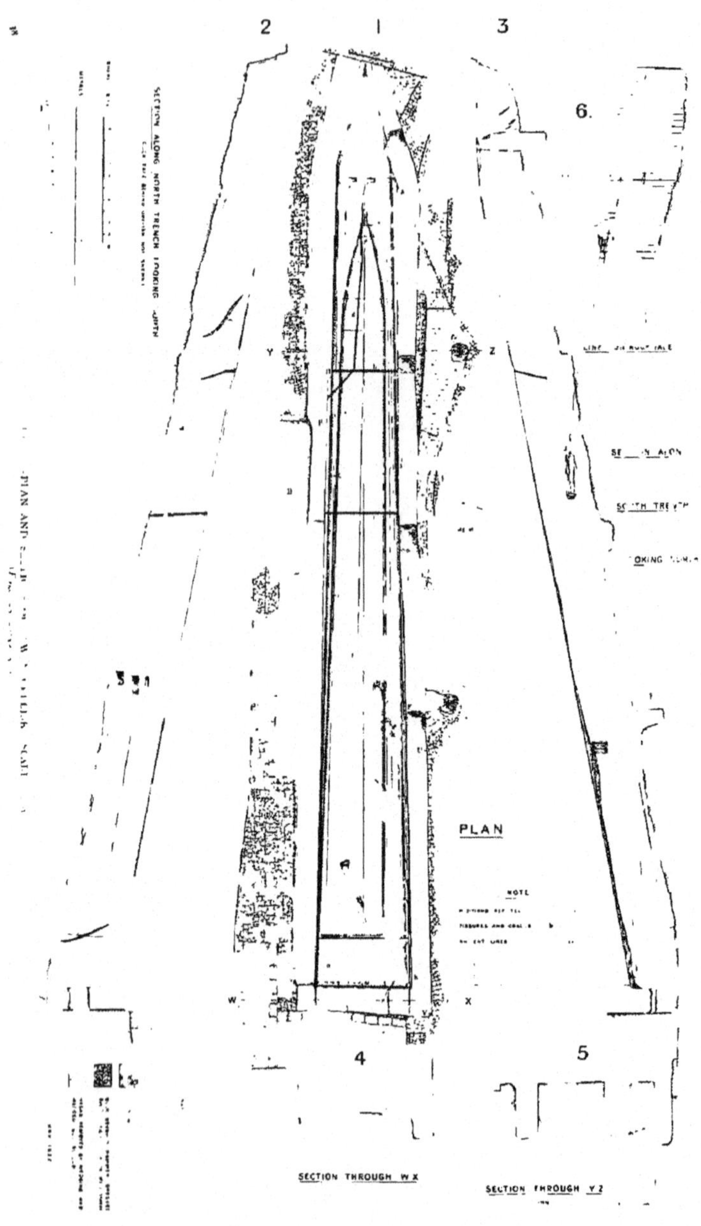

difference. It is clear, however, that the channels belong to the latter work. The probable explanation of them is that they are over discolorations in the granite, recognised as such and left by the original workmen.

Before we can say that we understand every step of the work so far, we have to inquire into the nature of the tools with which the wedge-slots were cut. This is a problem that has not been solved with certainty. Not only could the Egyptians cut granite with chisels, but they could cut even harder stones, such as diorite and quartzite. Though iron was known to them from the earliest times (but used rather sparingly), there is no evidence at all that steel was used; all the Egyptian words for metals have been accounted for, none of which could be applied to it. Another indication that steel was unknown is that razors, which are often found, are always of copper; had steel been known I think that razors would have surely been made of it. Copper, with 2 per cent. alloy, can be brought by hammering to the hardness of mild steel, and it seems within the bounds of possibility that the Egyptians could bring it to an even greater hardness.

Wilkinson, in his *Manners and Customs* II, page 255, cites an ancient chisel where the malletted end was worn by the blows, but where the cutting edge was sharp. This may well be explained by the fact that it had just been re-sharpened, but I have myself seen a chisel with the edge split like a modern machine-tool.

I was unable to purchase this specimen, but I tried the hardness with a knife and it was obvious that any great temper that it may once have possessed had disappeared. An examination of the structure of ancient copper chisels shows conclusively that the copper had never been raised to the annealing temperature.

It has been asserted that if the Egyptians had known steel it would have perished by oxydisation. This is not borne out by excavations, as many iron tools have been found, such as wedges, halberds, etc., which are hardly rusted at all. In some soils almost anything will be preserved; in others everything, except perhaps the pottery, perishes. An examination of such fragments of iron tools as can be spared might give us some definite information as to whether any of them were of steel and so settle a vexed question. I have spent hours trying to cut granite with iron, copper, and even dolerite chisels, and though granite can be cut—in a manner of speaking—with all of them I am convinced that the Egyptians used a much harder tool. There is still a great divergence of opinion on this subject, which is best left open until further evidence is forthcoming.

CHAPTER IV

EXTRACTION OF AN OBELISK

IN this chapter we are concerned with the formation of the obelisk and detaching it from the surrounding rock for transport. The surface of the rock is smooth and the work on the pits around the obelisk is well under weigh.

The next step seems to have been to mark on the surface of the rock the outline of the proposed obelisk. This must have been done by the normal Egyptian method of stretching a cord covered with ochre or lampblack over the proposed centre line and allowing the cord, when correctly placed, to touch the stone. The lines were next made permanent by scratching them with a metal tool. A pot containing red ochre was actually found during the clearance of the obelisk. The ochre or lampblack was probably mixed, before use, with acacia gum.

From this centre line, by measuring off, the corners of the pyramidion and base were correctly marked and joined up.

Let us examine the structure of the interior of the trench; we are struck with the absence of any marks of wedges or chisels. The ancient chisels leave traces which are easily recognisable (figs. 8 and 9), but here we have the effect of a series of parallel, vertical "cuts" just as if the rock had been extracted with a gigantic cheese-scoop. A further feature of the trench is that there are no corners—everything is rounded. These peculiarities are seen, not only in the trench, but in the pits within the trench and even the test-shafts C and D (fig. 7). The only tools which could produce this effect are the dolerite balls of which we have already made mention. The trench and pits were therefore not cut out, but rather bashed out. These balls measure from 5 to 12 inches in diameter, their weights averaging 12 pounds. They are of almost natural occurrence in some of the valleys in the eastern desert, having been shaped by the action of water in geological ages. A more economical or efficient tool can hardly be conceived. I have buried some hundreds of these behind the retaining wall, as even their size and weight did not protect them from souvenir-hunters.

The blows with these balls were struck vertically downwards, often with such force as to split them in two. This suggests that they were shod on to rammers, as it is almost impossible to break them by hand. The only way I succeeded in doing so was by pitching one down from a height on to a pile of others. This is further borne out by the fact that the wear on the balls is not even over the whole surface, but appears in patches, showing that they were used in one position until the bruising surface had become flat, and then changed to another position.

If we enter the trench we see that, down the division between each concave " cut," a red line has been drawn, apparently by means of a plumb-bob with its string dipped in ochre.

FIG. 8. WEDGE AND CHISEL MARKS NEAR ASWAN OBELISK.
(*Page* 31.)

FIG. 9. ROUGH CHISEL-DRESSING ON UNFINISHED SARCOPHAGI KNOWN AS "EL-HAMMÂMMÂT" NEAR ASWAN.
(*Page* 31.)

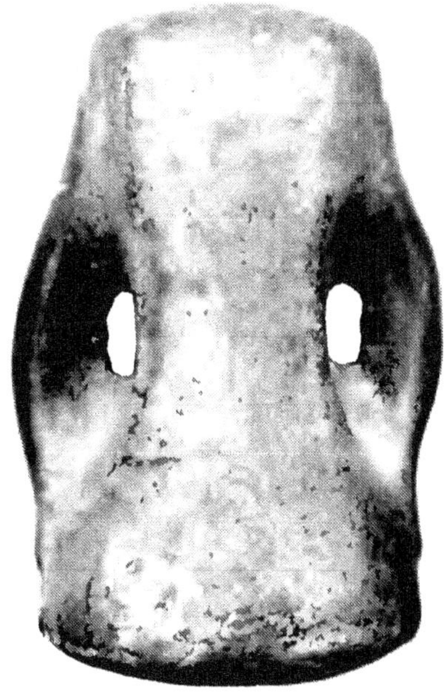

FIG. 10. BLACK GRANITE HAMMER FROM GIZEH.
(*Page* 34.)

FIG. 11. INTERIOR OF SEPARATING-TRENCH ROUND ASWAN OBELISK.
(*Pages 42 and 43.*)

FIG. 12.—VIEW OF TRENCH ROUND ASWAN OBELISK WHEN STANDING WITHIN IT.

These red lines are not continuous, but have been projected down from time to time as the bottom of the trench became deeper. The width between successive lines averages 11·77 inches, there being very little variation between examples. These divisions seem to be feet. The main measurements of the obelisk are based on the royal cubit of 20·71 inches. Whether this foot is intended to be on the same system as the royal cubit I am not certain. The following table shows that it can be referred to it with tolerable closeness :—

Finger	.. (1) ..	.. ·74 inches.
Palm	.. (4) ..	.. 2·95 ,,
Foot	.. (16) ..	.. 11·81 ,,
Common cubit	.. (24) ..	.. 17·71 ,,
Royal cubit ..	.. (28) ..	.. 20·67 ,,

Looking down the trench (fig. 11) we see that it is divided into a right and left half; further, from the upper quarry-face (fig. 13, p. 44), it can be seen that the vertical measuring "chains" described on page 46 only occur every two feet-divisions along the trench. The most reasonable explanation of this seems to be that each man or party of men were given two feet of trench as their task, and that they worked it from each side of the trench alternately. Some 130 men could work in the bottom of the trench at the same time, possibly assisted by 260 more working the rammers (p. 42) from above. When the granite is broken up by means of the dolerite balls or "pounders" it comes away in the form of powder and not as flakes. If the powder is not removed every few minutes, it soon forms a cushion, and the effect of the blows is reduced almost to nil. Handing the powder out of the trench would be a great waste of time, so it seems most likely that it was brushed on to the part of the task which was not being pounded; that is, each man worked on his task in four positions, with his back to, and facing, the obelisk on his right and left foot of trench. There is only one way by which such a large number of men can work in so confined a space without interfering with one another, and that is by making each man work in the same relative position on his task, and when a change in the position is required, by letting it be simultaneous. We have no means of knowing at what intervals of time these changes were made.

Nowadays work with rammers or mindalah's, as the modern Egyptians call them, is always done to a sort of chanty, and there is ample evidence that the ancients made similar use of songs to help them in their labours. We can easily picture some ancient, leather-lunged foreman bawling out a prototype of the modern *mindalah* song:—

(Chorus) *Ya* Sayyid hizz *il*[1]-Hilâl
(Foreman) M' Is*kin*diria *lish*-Shellâl
(Chorus) *Ya* Sayyid hizz *il*-Hilâl
(Foreman) *Duqq'* y' awlâd khabar *eyh* ummâl?

O Sayyid, brandish the Crescent!
From Alexandria to the Cataract.
O Sayyid, brandish the Crescent!
Bash, boys, what's up with you?

[1] The curious fall of the beat may horrify the Arabic scholar, but this is the way I have so often heard it.

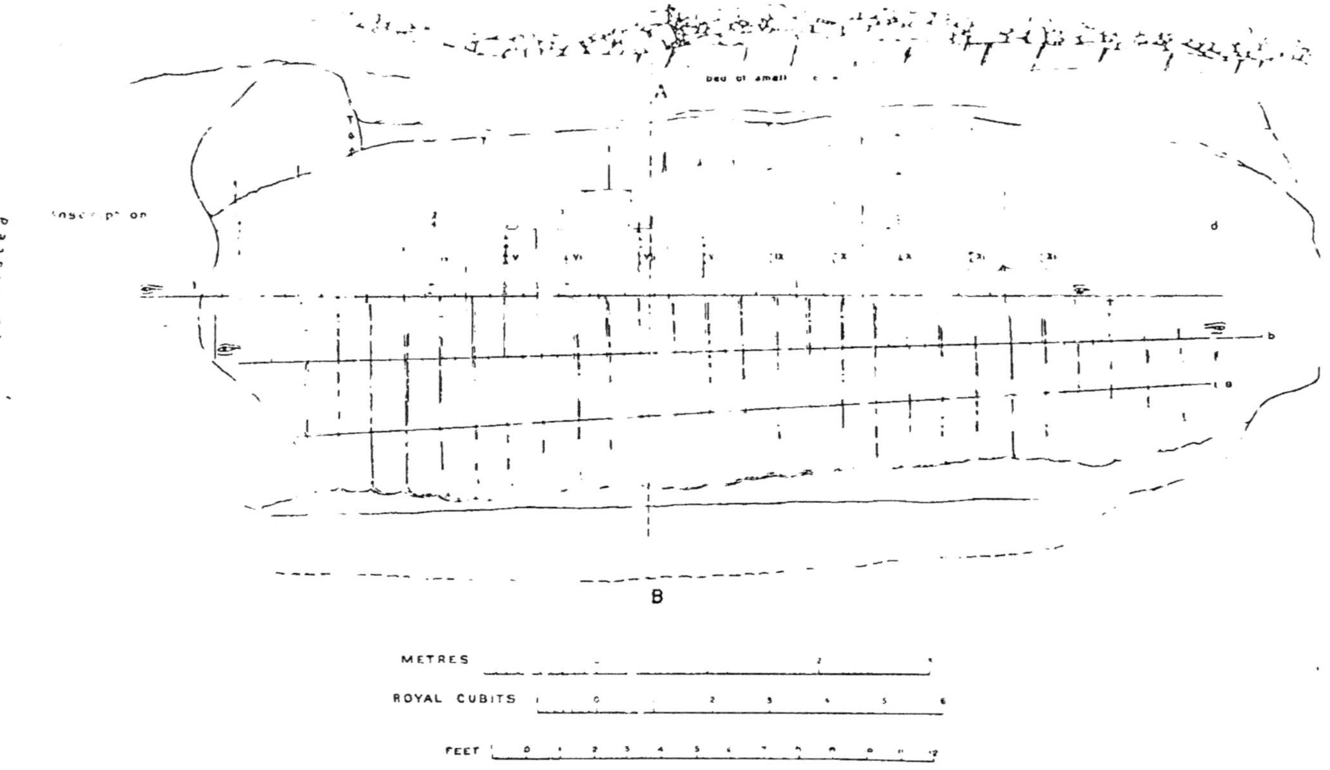

FIG. 13.—MEASURING-LINES ON UPPER QUARRY FACE ASWAN OBELISK

(*Page* 4, 40 *and* 5)

with 130—perhaps 390—men pounding out the beat. With a good chanter who can extemporise rhyming lines full of highly-flavoured personalities, the work the Egyptian can do is little short of marvellous, but with a bad one the tune soon degenerates into a kind of *andante religioso*, resulting in remarks from the Director of Works of quite the reverse kind. This is, however, by the way.

The average width of the trench is about 2 feet 6 inches, and it is possible that the workmen were given a minimum width; but this is not necessarily the case, as it would be false economy to make the trench too narrow, since the cramped position of the man in the trench would prevent him getting the best force in his blows, besides tending to make him pound his own toes instead of the rock. In some places the trench, after narrowing as it gets deeper, suddenly widens out again. I explain these narrowings—best seen at Z on fig. 7—by the fact that the work of a particular shift was to end at that level, which they tried to reach quickly, knowing that others had to continue it.

When one considers the cramped position of the men pounding out the pits along the line of the proposed trench in the initial stages of the work, it can easily be understood how soon the trench parties overhauled them (p. 35). The work on the original test-shafts must have been even slower still.

As to the manner of measuring up the work, which was almost certainly done by forced labour—some sort of corvée perhaps—helped out by such troops and captives as were available, I am convinced that it was by piece and not by time. In the obelisk trench, the work appears to have been measured by the foreman with a scaled rod, from the various red and black horizontal lines seen in great profusion on the sides of the trench (for examples see fig. 7, no. 6). In the work on the monument which has been removed from before the upper quarry-face (fig. 13), it seems that the work was measured up after every two or three days' pounding from

FIG. 14. FIG. 15. FIG. 16. FIG. 17.
TRACES OF INSCRIPTIONS ON UPPER QUARRY-FACE.

the bottom of the trench by means of a rod of three cubits length, and the position of the top of the rod marked with a short horizontal red line, which was connected to the previous mark by an inverted Y. This seems the only explanation of the curious red chains seen faintly in the middle of the two-foot tasks. The half-effaced chains higher up seem to be the records of the preceding shifts. These appear to have been distinguished by short inscriptions scrawled by them in red paint. Most of these inscriptions are too faint to transcribe. Figs. 14–15, from the right of the chains in divisions VIII, IX and XII respectively, and fig. 17, from the left of the red chain of division VIII, are the most complete and clear, but they are too fragmentary to translate. They may originally have given some information as to the party engaged in their division. At the extreme left of the upper quarry-face there are traces of a hieratic inscription of two lines which I have not been able to decipher nor to photograph with any clearness. It is in black paint, and appears to begin with a date and to have a number in the middle, but does not give any royal name.

It is rather tempting to see, in the black lines *a* and *c* (fig. 13) on the upper quarry-face, the top and bottom faces of a small obelisk with *b* as its centre line. If this is so, the taper is 1 in 17·5, which is sharper than other obelisks. Line *c* is very nearly level, and both *b* and *c* are divided into feet by short black vertical lines in the middle of the pounded-out grooves. The reason of this is not clear to me, neither have I been able to find any explanation of the red line *d*, which is separated from the line *a* by 2 feet, nor for the eyes and other signs which occur at various places on the face of the rock. The red *nefer* sign under the eye just after division XIII is usually used to mean "ground level" in other quarries, but it certainly has not that meaning here, though it may well indicate that line *c*, at the top of the sign, is meant to be level.

To return to the trench, it is interesting to speculate on the amount of time which was expended in making it. To ascertain this, I tried pounding for an hour by hand at various times on one of the quarters of a two-foot task, and I found that I had reduced the level by about 5 millimetres (·2 inches) average. With practice I could perhaps have done more. Let us assume that the ancients could extract 8 millimetres (3·15 inches) per hour from a similar area; then the time taken to make the trench must be that taken to do the deepest part. In this obelisk the trench would have to be 165 inches to make it of square cross-section and we must allow at least 40 inches for under-cutting (p. 49), making a total depth of trench required of 205 inches. Supposing that 3·15 inches were extracted from a quarter of each party's task per hour, it will require $\frac{4 \times 205}{3{\cdot}15 \times 12 \times 30}$ or 7·2 months of twelve hours per day. The under-cutting would have taken at least as long again, even though it could be done from both sides at once.

Before leaving the subject of the time taken, let us apply the results obtained from my pounding experiments to the obelisk of Queen Hatshepsôwet at Karnak, of which the measurements are given on page 30. To the base measurement of 94 inches we must add, say,

30 inches for under-cutting, making a total depth required of 124 inches. Calculating in the same way as before, we find the time necessary would be 4·4 months, working twelve hours a day. For detaching it from below we may add a similar period, making 8·8 months.

It is recorded by the Queen that " they are of one block of enduring granite, without seam or joining. My Majesty exacted work thereon from the year 15, the first of the sixth month until the year 16, the last day of the twelfth month, making seven months of exaction in the quarry."[1] If the men were worked in continuous shifts, this work could have easily been done in the time she mentions, even if the Egyptians were not able to break up the granite at a much greater rate than I was able to do. At the foot of the standing obelisk at Karnak, where her inscription appears, she implores us not to say " it is a lie ! " but rather " how like her ! " The calculation above at any rate tends to give her the benefit of the doubt.

The only evidence we have as to how the obelisk was separated from the rock beneath it is to be found above the upper quarry-face, where there is a bed from which a monument 22 feet long has been removed (shown in fig. 19, p. 50). The bottom of the trench around it can still be traced, and the two-foot divisions are

[1] The months refer to the absolute year. The regnal year 15 happens to end in the middle of the period referred to. Hence the apparent error in the number of months stated. It is a quite correct total. For complete translation see page 102.

of the same size as those of the great obelisk. Here it is quite clear that the detaching from below was done also by pounding. In the work below the monument, though the two-foot divisions of each party's task are rigidly maintained, the sub-divisions into a right and left half have become very irregular, which is what would be expected in work under such conditions. A curious fact is that the monument has been snapped off when the workers on each side had nearly met. Whether this was intentional or not cannot be known, but it seems more likely that it was accidental. With regard to a large obelisk, I think we may safely say that it was neither snapped off its bed nor removed by the action of wedges from both sides. In a very long monument, the strains set up by the uneven expansions of the wedges, some biting true and some slipping out and not acting at all, would probably crack the monument in two, especially in the case of an obelisk like this, which could only safely stand the strains due to its own weight (p. 75). It is fairly safe to assume that all large monuments were completely detached, perhaps by driving a series of galleries through first, packing them well by wood or stone as near the centre of the monument as possible, and then removing the remainder of the rock. There is no evidence at all as to the nature of the packing.

At the west end of the ridge from which the small monument has been removed there is a short inscription in red paint. It seems to begin

Fig. 18.—VIEW OF ASWAN OBELISK FROM THE NORTH.
(*Pages 26 and 33.*)

Fig. 19.—BED FROM WHICH A SMALL MONUMENT, PROBABLY AN OBELISK, HAS BEEN REMOVED.
(*Page 49.*)

with the words "The work of," followed by a group of signs which are not intelligible to me. It seems that the last group of signs are not hieroglyphs at all. Such illegible groups are not rare in quarries.

During the clearance of the obelisk, part of a letter on a piece of pottery was found. Though extremely fragmentary, there was a remark on it about "beating" the stone. This may well refer to the pounding process by which the monuments were extracted.

CHAPTER V

TRANSPORT OF AN OBELISK

IN the last chapter we discussed the methods by which the quarrying was performed. The next step was the removal of the obelisk from the quarry, and its transport to the river and thence by water to its destination.

It might be remarked that the Aswan obelisk —the largest known—has *not* been transported, but I think we are justified in assuming that the man responsible for the work would never have begun on it had he not every reason to believe that he could carry it out. Judging from such sketches as have come down to us of the character of Egyptian kings, they were not likely to tolerate a failure, unless it was from some unavoidable cause. We must bear in mind, too, that the ancient engineers moved blocks as heavy as this obelisk, and even more unmanageable—the colossi of Amenophis III and the colossus of Ramesses II at Thebes. We shall, therefore, take the Aswan obelisk as the basis of our speculations as, if we can account for every step in its history from the quarry to the temple, we can account for that of any other obelisk. The converse, reasoning from a small obelisk, would not necessarily be true.

The obelisk, then, is lying on its packing surrounded by the trench, but detached from the parent rock.

If we look at the surface of the rock outside the north (valley side) trench, we see that its level is the same as that of the surface of the obelisk. The parts A and B (fig. 7, p. 38) have most certainly been removed at a later date than the rest. It seems that a surface of rock, running continuously along the outside of the trench at the same level as that of the obelisk, was purposely left. It might be urged that this is merely the remainder of the flattened surface on which the obelisk was set out (p. 36). This may well be the case, but if we consider in detail how the obelisk was to be got out of the pit in which it lies, factors arise which point to a very definite reason for leaving this surface as it now is.

There are two methods by which the obelisk can be removed from its present position: one is by raising it, and the other is by removing the rock from in front of it; sliding it out endways is impossible in this particular case. It may be mentioned here that to pull the obelisk over, on a level surface, would require some 13,000 men, which I am convinced could not be put on ropes in the constricted area of the quarry. To roll it out as it is would require an enormous quantity of rock to be removed, and one would think that, if they intended to use this method, they would have begun to do so as soon as possible. The fact remains, however, that they have not begun to do this, though they are well on with the breaking up of the rock (B, fig. 22, p. 60) to let the tip of the obelisk pass out.

This piece of rock is also to be seen in fig. 8, p. 42.

A combination of both methods seems to have been intended, and the reason for leaving the north trench intact was for the use of large vertical levers. These would probably be tree-trunks, some two feet in diameter and 20 or more feet long, inserted, with suitable packing, in the trench, with many men pulling on ropes attached to the top of them. It seems that the workmen had begun to reduce the rock on the quarry side of the obelisk as well, so that levers could be used from there also. By using these levers from both sides of the obelisk in turn, it could be made to rock slightly backwards and forwards and gradually be raised by increasing the height of the packing below at each heave. By this means the base could be raised some 8 feet above its present level, and the quantity of rock to be removed from in front of the obelisk greatly reduced in consequence.

As to the numbers of levers needed; it can easily be calculated that, if they used thirty 20-foot tree-trunks at a leverage of six to one, with 50 men pulling on the ropes at the top of each, the obelisk would move, and the wood—whether it was of fir, cypress or sycomore-fig—would not be unduly strained. This is a conservative figure, and I think it likely that they would have used much taller trunks with at least 100 men pulling on each. On the further side of the obelisk, a comparatively small amount of rock would have to be removed in order to use the levers as, if they can move some 20 degrees back from the vertical, a sufficient rise in that side of the obelisk could be obtained. As the base of the obelisk became higher, rock would have to be packed behind the levers, and on the valley side this would have to be very considerable, though with only 100 men per lever they could be used at a slope.

As to the problem of packing the levers and keeping them steady, this is merely a matter of head-ropes and foot-ropes and could have been done in many ways. I do not propose to speculate on which particular method the Egyptians used, as there is no evidence on the subject.

Directly the obelisk had been raised as high as possible, the destruction of the rock in front of it would be done by wedging and burning, as described in Chapter III. I should think that it would be removed until there was a considerable slope downwards to the valley below, which would greatly reduce the number of men required to roll it. At the last heave of the levers from the valley side, the packing could be entirely withdrawn, and sand substituted; this could be gradually removed, and the obelisk allowed to settle down on to its edge and a great saving of men effected in this, its first and most difficult turn. By judiciously introducing a bank of sand where the middle of the face of the obelisk was to come, and by digging below its edge, the rolling could be made to approximate to that of a cylinder and its downward journey rendered comparatively easy.

The ropes for rolling the obelisk out would be passed round it and brought out to anchorages in front. I believe that 40 7¼-inch palm ropes (or their equivalent), pulled by 6,000 men, would be sufficient to handle the obelisk in any stage of its removal down the valley. Such large ropes would have to be pulled by handling-loops. In the scene of the transport of a great winged bull at Nineveh, they can be seen passing over the men's shoulders, being attached at both ends to the main cable. In a photograph in *Wonders of the Past*, page 421 (Harmsworth Encyclopedias), these loops can be seen very clearly.

The occurrence of levers is so rare that it has been doubted whether the Egyptians knew of them. I think that there is not the slightest doubt that they did know of them, as in the temples of the Theban area and in the temple of the third pyramid at Gizeh, one can see large blocks, undercut at various points along their length, obviously to take the points of levers. In a tomb at El-Bersheh (*Annales du Service des Antiquités*, I, p. 28), an acacia branch, with its end cut to a chisel edge, was found, which must have been used to manipulate the lid of the sarcophagus. It might be asked why no very large levers have been found. The reason is that large baulks would not be abandoned in the quarry, but would be used until they were no longer sound, and then cut up and re-used for other purposes. Like timber baulks to-day, they were of considerable value, and not thrown away when a job was completed. The Assyrians, at any rate, knew them, for in a sculpture of about the VIIIth century B.C. there is a scene of men hauling along a colossal bull mounted on a sled running on rollers, with men overcoming the initial friction with levers from behind (Layard, *Discoveries*, Plates X–XVII).

We know, from the celebrated sculpture at Dêr El-Bahari, that the obelisks of Queen

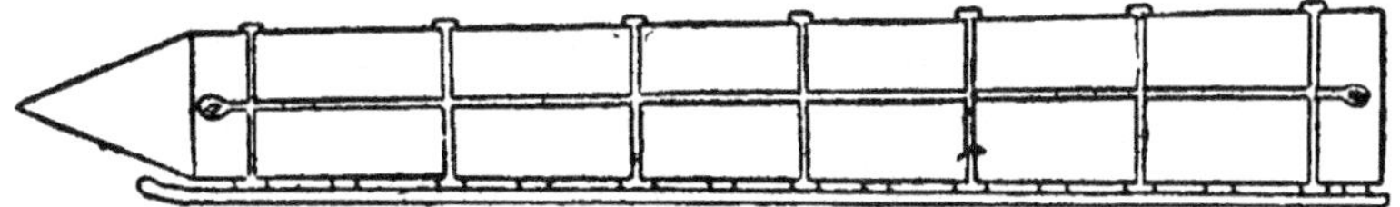

FIG. 20.—OBELISK OF HATSHEPSÔWET, MOUNTED ON A SLED, FROM HER SCULPTURES AT DÊR EL-BAHARI.

Hatshepsôwet were transported on sleds. Fig. 20 is taken from the transport scene. It was probably done by the court artist from memory, and though the general impression is most likely correct, several of the details appear to be wrong. Thus he slurs over the manner in which the baulks of timber at the top of the obelisk were attached to those on the sled, which must have been done by the known Egyptian method of the "Spanish windlass," that is, by passing ropes round corresponding baulks and tightening them after the manner of a tourniquet (fig. 28, p. 70). The position of the hauling-rope in the centre of the obelisk must also surely be wrong, as that would be the very worst position for pulling the obelisk; the rope would, of course, be attached to the sled, as it is shown in other similar scenes which have come down to us. It seems likely too that the obelisk was really on the sled the reverse way round (p. 70). The fact that the Dêr El-Bahari obelisks were mounted on sleds is no proof that all obelisks were so mounted for transport, but I think it most likely that they were, as without a sled it would be extremely difficult to attach ropes to the obelisk so as to be able to pull it lengthways; further, a sled would be an excellent shock-absorber and would equalise the upward pressure of the rollers along the length of the obelisk. This is almost a necessity in such a long obelisk as this, as, if it came down on a roller near its centre with a jerk, it would snap in two (p. 75).

Next comes the vexed question whether rollers were used in conjunction with the sled or not. It has been assumed by certain writers, because in the tomb scene of the transport of the 60-ton statue of Dhuthotpe at El-Bersheh (Lepsius, *Denkmäler*, II, 134, and p. 59) the sled was merely pulled over a wetted track, that all blocks were so transported, whatever their size. When it is realised that it took 172 men—who would pull about 8 tons—to haul this statue, one hesitates to assert that a block of 1,170 tons was so handled. Caution is very necessary, but to deny that rollers were known in Egypt, as some writers would have us do, is either to invite far less justifiable assumptions, or to bring all reasoning to a standstill. The 227-ton obelisk now in Paris, when it was being pulled up a slight slope, mounted on a sled or " cradle " sliding over a greased way, required a pull of 94 tons. To handle the Aswan obelisk in this way would take at least 11,000 men, which is

FIG. 21.—TRANSPORT OF THE STATUE OF DHUTHOTPE, FROM HIS TOMB AT EL-BERSHEH.

outside the bounds of possibility, if only from considerations of space. Small rollers have actually been found, but no large ones, for reasons already given for the absence of large levers. It is rather difficult to obtain data as to the size of rollers required for such an obelisk as that of Aswan. The only information I can give is that the top of the fallen obelisk of Queen Hapshepsôwet rests on 8-inch diameter pitch-pine rollers, spaced about a yard apart, and there is no sign of any crushing, though they have been there for many years. The worst pressure at that spacing which they would have to bear at the butt-end of the Aswan obelisk, if it were placed on them for transport, would not exceed 11 times the amount they bear now.

The process of putting the obelisk on to its sled and rollers must have been something of this kind: at the foot of the slope leading down from the quarry the sled—mounted on its rollers and track baulks—would be buried, sighting-poles being put in to mark the position of its axis. The obelisk would then be rolled down the slope until it lay exactly over the sled, and the sand dug away till the obelisk settled down on to it. After digging the sled clear, the journey to the river could be begun, the track being packed as hard as possible, most probably with baulks of timber laid down lengthways on which the rollers could run. The route for the Aswan obelisk would almost certainly have been north-eastwards along the track of the old Barrage railway (D–A, fig. 22, and fig. 26, p. 70), until it joined the embankment F–E which leads to the river. Its exact point of arrival at the Nile is hidden by the modern town.

On the details of the enormous barges on which obelisks are known to have been transported,

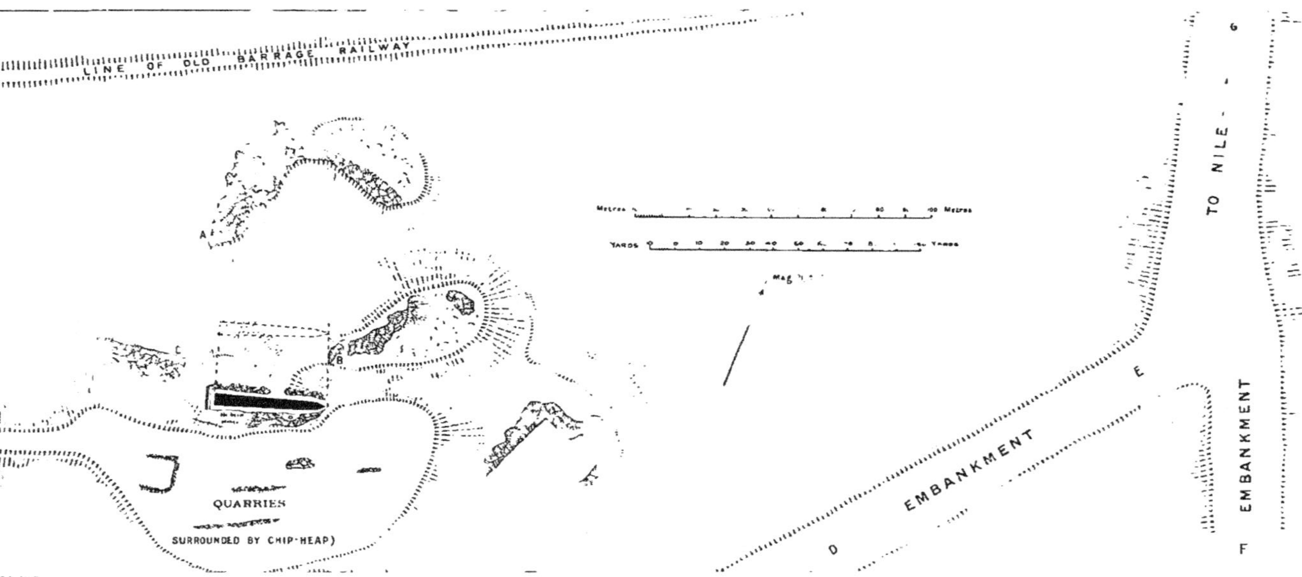

FIG. 12.—SKETCH-PLAN OF THE NEIGHBOURHOOD OF OBELISK QUARRY, ASWAN

I have to be more than vague, as the only scene of a boat sufficiently large to carry an obelisk is that on the Dêr El-Bahari sculpture, where the two obelisks—probably those now seen at Karnak—are both placed butt to butt on the same barge! The boat used must have been over 200 feet in length. Another great barge is mentioned (p. 94) measuring 207 feet long by 69 feet broad, which carried the two obelisks

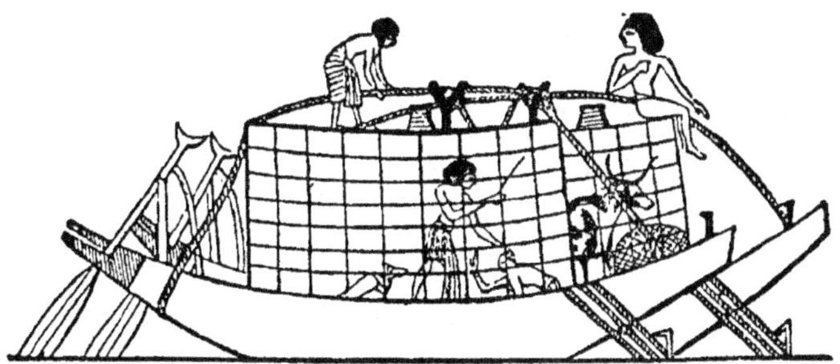

FIG. 23.—CARGO-BOAT, NEW KINGDOM.

of Tuthmôsis I, and we have a record of a third boat in the Old Kingdom, made by one Uni of the VIth dynasty, which was 102 feet long, and which took only 17 days to build (Breasted, *Ancient Records*, I, 322, and II, 105).

Mr. Somers Clarke, in *Ancient Egypt*, 1920, Parts 1 and 2 (Macmillan; 2*s.* quarterly), has collected all known facts on the construction of ancient boats. He admits that the details of the very large ships are quite unknown, as the Dêr El-Bahari boat already referred to is only, as it were, an impressionist view, and from it we can learn little of its internal structure.

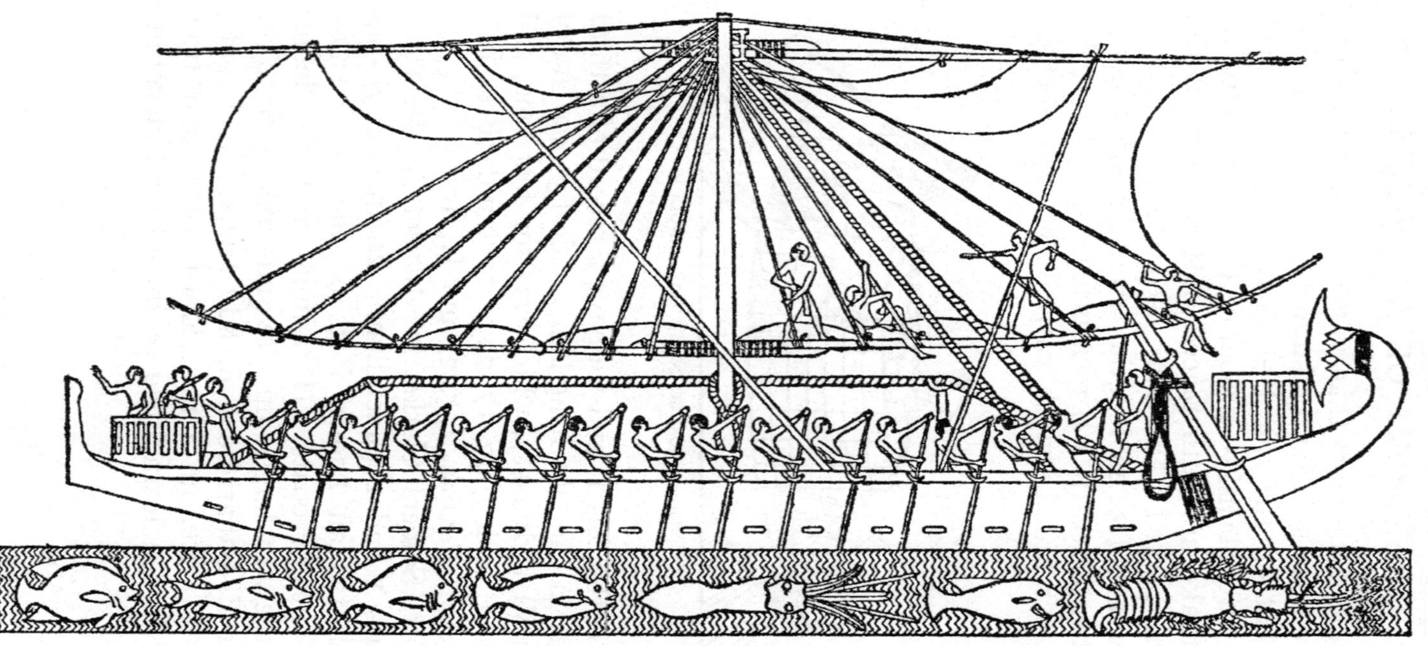

Fig. 24.—BOAT OF QUEEN HATSHEPSOWET FROM THE PUNT RELIEFS AT DÊR EL-BAHARI

The ancient boats in the Cairo Museum are only of quite small size ; these are built without ribs, but whether the obelisk-barges were of this type also is uncertain. The Dêr El-Bahari boats are stiffened by means of a series of ropes attached to the bow and stern, passing over vertical supports at two points in the body of the boat, thus forming what is now known as a queen-truss or hog-frame. This method of stiffening is well shown in figs. 23 and 24. It is better to leave the question of the large boats until further evidence is forthcoming, but before doing so I will give a passage in Mr. Clarke's article which is of interest to the general reader. He says, quoting from a letter from the late Mr. Francis Elgar, Director of Naval Construction to the British Government: " The two great obelisks of Karnak, 97 feet 6 inches long, could be carried on a boat about 220 feet long and 69 feet beam, upon a draught of water of about 4 feet 6 inches or not exceeding 5 feet." Some of the large Cook's boats approach this length, but their beam is very different. Mr. Clarke remarks later: " Whence came the necessary knowledge, at what period did the people begin to accumulate the experience, which culminated in their power to deal with immense weights . . . not only in the XIIth and XVIIIth dynasties, but in the IIIrd and IVth ? "

It is a very great pity that the scenes of the transport by boat of Hatshepsôwet's obelisks are not accompanied by a real descriptive text. All that we can learn from the inscriptions is that the boat was built of sycomore-fig, and the fact that a whole army was mustered at Elephantine, or Aswan, to load the obelisks on to it. There is plenty also about the rejoicings of the priests, marines and recruits over their arrival at Thebes. The scenes themselves, however, show us that the obelisk-barge was towed by three rows of oared tow-boats, which were arranged nine in a row, each row being led by a pilot-boat. Near the great barge are three boats escorting it, in which religious ceremonies are apparently being performed. We see the troops on the shore waiting to do the unloading, and an offering being performed by officials and priests. The name of the King, Tuthmôsis III, is mentioned in the laudatory sentences after the Queen. In the view of the great barge, which is badly damaged, the obelisks are placed high up on her deck. This is possibly a trick by the artist so that they may be visible.

There is only one practical way of putting a large obelisk into a barge, and that is by getting the boat as close to the bank as possible, building an embankment round and over it, and pulling the obelisk directly over the boat and letting it down into its place by digging out the filling from beneath it. Possibly a new set of baulks and rollers were already prepared inside the barge. The boat would then be dug clear and the journey by water made. Though I see no reason to suppose that the rise and fall of the Nile were used for the loading and unloading of the boat, it is more than probable that it was arranged that the water journey was made at high Nile to minimise the risk of running aground.

The unloading would be a rather simpler matter. An embankment would be constructed from the shore to the boat (and around it), but only reaching to the level of the rollers of the obelisk. The boat would be destroyed—or at least the prow removed—and the journey continued towards the temple.

CHAPTER VI

ERECTION OF OBELISKS

THE ancient method of setting up a large obelisk has been a fruitful subject for speculation for generations, and many extraordinary theories have been put forward by archæologists, engineers, architects, and that bane of the serious student, the reckless exponent of the occult.

In mediæval and modern times, the erection of an obelisk has always involved capstans or winches actuating a system of pulleys, and in most cases a "jack"—either hydraulic or screw—has had to be called into use. It is generally admitted that the Egyptians were not familiar either with the screw-jack, capstan, winch or the system of pulleys arranged to give a mechanical advantage; it is even debatable whether they knew the simple pulley.

Sheers (see fig. 41, p. 116) were possibly known in principle, though we have no proof of it, but the erection of an obelisk by this means must involve the use of the capstan or winch.

This leaves levers as the only source of power except the employment of large numbers of men. We have therefore to try and explain how the large obelisks were erected by these means only.

Two theories stand out as being reasonable, though both leave a good deal unexplained.

One is that the edge of the obelisk was placed so as to engage in the narrow notch which always runs along one side of the surface of the pedestals (see fig. 25, A–B), and that it was gradually levered up, the earth being banked behind the levers at each heave, until the obelisk was leaning against an earth slope at a sufficiently steep angle to permit it to be easily pulled upright. This method was actually used for the erection of the memorial obelisk of Seringapatam, but the obelisk only weighed some 35 tons. Some of the reasons against this having been the Egyptian method are as follows :—

(*a*) The Egyptians could introduce obelisks inside courts whose walls were shorter than the length of the obelisk. Queen Hatshepsôwet put hers between her father's pylons where there was a court of Osirid figures, and there is no evidence at all that any of the walls had been removed or rebuilt ; in fact I am certain that they were not.

(*b*) Some obelisks are so close to their pylons that there would hardly be room for the huge levers which would have had to be used.

(*c*) After pulling the obelisk upright there is nothing to stop it from rocking about and getting out of control. The lowering of the New York obelisk (p. 118) showed clearly that, once it was on the move, head-ropes were more than unreliable in checking the momentum of such a mass.

(*d*) The obelisk of Hatshepsôwet at Karnak has come on to its pedestal askew (see fig. 25), and has never used the notch at all, as its edge is quite sharp and unburred. This shows that the notch—an essential for this method—was not an essential for the ancient method.

The other theory is that the obelisk was pulled up a long sloping embankment until it was at a height well above that of its balancing-point or "centre of gravity," and that earth was cut from below it carefully until the obelisk settled down on to the pedestal with its edge in the pedestal-notch, leaning, as in the last method, against the end of the embankment. From thence it was pulled upright.

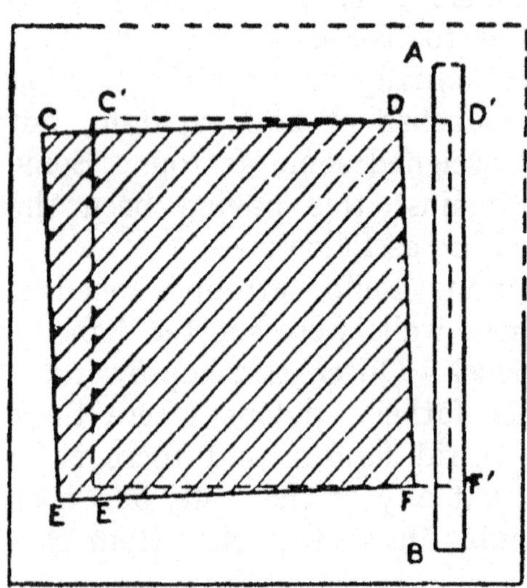

Fig. 25.
POSITION OF THE BASE OF HATSHEPSÔWET'S OBELISK ON ITS PEDESTAL.

The use of a large sloping embankment is more than likely, as (see note *a* above) the obelisk was obviously lowered on to its pedestal and not raised at all; this method, however, has some serious objections, which may be summed up briefly:

(*a*) It would be extremely risky business to cut earth from below an overhanging obelisk of 500 tons and upwards. Anyone who has seen earth undercut below a large stone in excavating work or elsewhere knows that the earth has a partiality for slipping sideways in any direction but the expected—preferably on to the heads of one's workmen.

(*b*) To make an obelisk settle down from a height on to a small pedestal by under-cutting would be an impossibility. Whatever method the Egyptians used, it was *certain*, and did not depend on the skill of the men with the pick and basket.

(*c*) See note *c* on the levering-up theory, which is equally applicable here.

A method which is mechanically possible and which meets all observed facts is that the obelisk was not let down over the edge of an embankment, but down a funnel-shaped pit *in* the end of it, the lowering being done by removing sand, with which the pit had been filled, from galleries leading into the bottom of it, and so allowing the obelisk to settle slowly down. Taking this as the basis of the method, the form of the pit resolves itself into a tapering square-sectioned funnel—rather like a petrol-funnel—fairly wide at the top, but very little larger than the base of the obelisk at the bottom. The obelisk is introduced into the funnel on a curved way leading gradually from the surface of the embankment until it engages smoothly with the hither wall of the funnel. The sand is removed by men with baskets through galleries leading from the bottom of the funnel to convenient places outside the embankment. Fig. 27 shows a model of such an embankment, in which the proportions of the obelisk and pylon are the same as those of the temple of Luxor. The opening in the front of the embankment at ground level leads into the bottom of the left wall of the funnel inside, entering just above the pedestal, over which the funnel is built. In this photograph the slope of the surface of the embankment is somewhat exaggerated; in reality it must have been very gradual, like that shown in fig. 26. The model of the embankment is almost exactly a $\frac{1}{1000}$ scale model of that which is given in the Anastasi Papyrus (see p. 89). The obelisk, which is of limestone, is a $\frac{1}{1000}$ scale model of the Aswan obelisk. By a curious coincidence they seem suitable to each other.

In fig. 28, the obelisk has arrived at the top of the slope and is overhanging the sand in the funnel. The model is made sectional as far as the funnel is concerned, and it must be imagined that a portion of the side of the embankment has been removed in order to show what is going on inside. A vertical sheet of glass has been put in the place of what would have been the front wall of the funnel to keep the sand from pouring out.

As to how the sled was separated from the obelisk I am not certain; it matters the less since there are several simple ways by which this can be done. In this series of photographs

FIG. 26.—GIGANTIC EMBANKMENT FOR TRANSPORTING STONE, ASWAN.
(*Pages 31 and 70.*)

FIG. 27.—SECTIONAL MODEL OF AN EMBANKMENT, TO SHOW METHOD OF ERECTING OBELISKS.
(*Page 70.*)

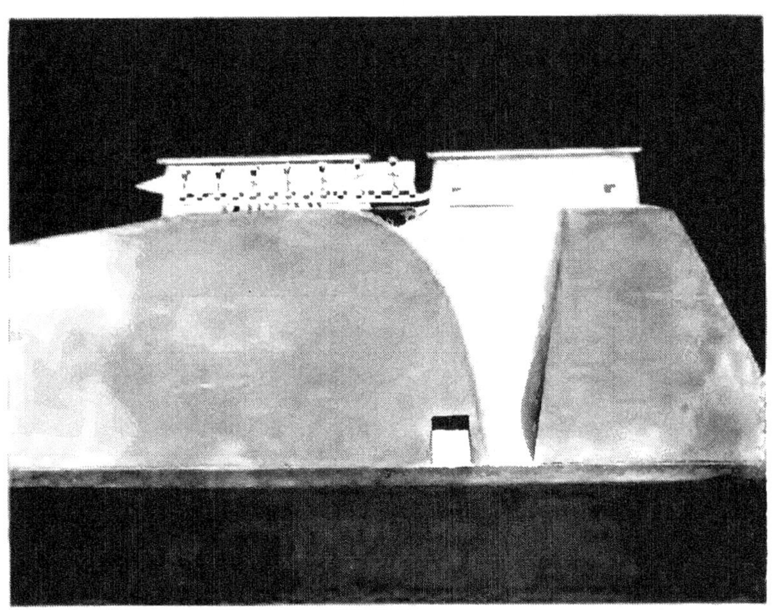

Fig. 28.—OBELISK AT THE TOP OF THE SLOPE, OVERHANGING THE SAND-FUNNEL.
(*Page* 70.)

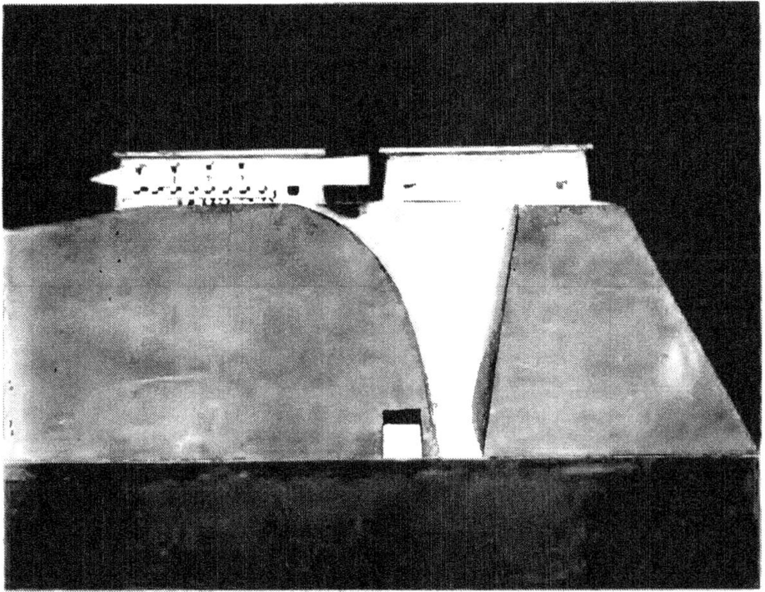

Fig. 29.—SLED HALF REMOVED.
(*Page* 71.)

the simplest method has been used, though I do not in any way insist that it was the ancient way.

In fig. 29 the overhanging part of the sled has been removed, and in fig. 30 the obelisk has been allowed to slide forward into the sand, and the attachments of the hind part of the sled taken away. Though this method would be quite suitable for any of the standing obelisks of Egypt, in the case of the Aswan obelisk, where the least jerk would be fatal, I imagine that the obelisk would be rolled on baulks right over the sand, and the sled, baulks and rollers cut and dug away, a rather more tedious process. It has been suggested to me that the obelisk and sled went down the funnel together. My objection to this is that a heavy obelisk and the light sled would part company on the way down, especially since the sled would be held back in the initial stages of the descent by the very great friction against the curve leading into the funnel. It would also be a difficult matter to gauge the exact position of the pedestal-notch so that the edge of the obelisk should engage in it.

Fig. 31 shows the obelisk on its way down. In this model, the sand was not actually removed through the galleries at the front and end of the embankment, but was allowed to run out through a slit—placed where the pedestal-notch should be—in the bottom of the funnel, directly under its left wall. The descent of the obelisk in the model is quite automatic, and it comes down every time as shown in fig. 32, but in an actual erection the rate of descent would be much slower and the flow of the sand, which in the model produces a decided dynamic effect, would be absent. It is more than probable therefore that men would go down with the obelisk and, by digging, correct any tendency of the obelisk to lean sideways and to ensure—if necessary by inserting baulks (struts) between the base of the obelisk and the opposite wall of the funnel—that it did not jam against it. After the position shown in fig. 31 had been passed, there would be little fear of a jam. It seems to have been neglect of these precautions which allowed Hatshepsôwet's standing obelisk at Karnak to come down too far forward, and so miss the notch on the pedestal altogether (fig. 25, p. 68).

The obelisk should come to rest as shown in fig. 32, lying flat against the left wall of the funnel. I have made several experiments in the slope of the sides of the funnel and the form of the leading-in curve, and I find that a wide range of variation will produce the desired results. The only necessity appears to be that the left wall of the funnel must be straight until it is of a height of at least two-thirds the height of the balancing-point of the obelisk before the curve begins.

If the position of the bottom of the funnel as regards the pedestal is so arranged that the notch in the latter comes directly under the left wall, the obelisk will come down on to the interior

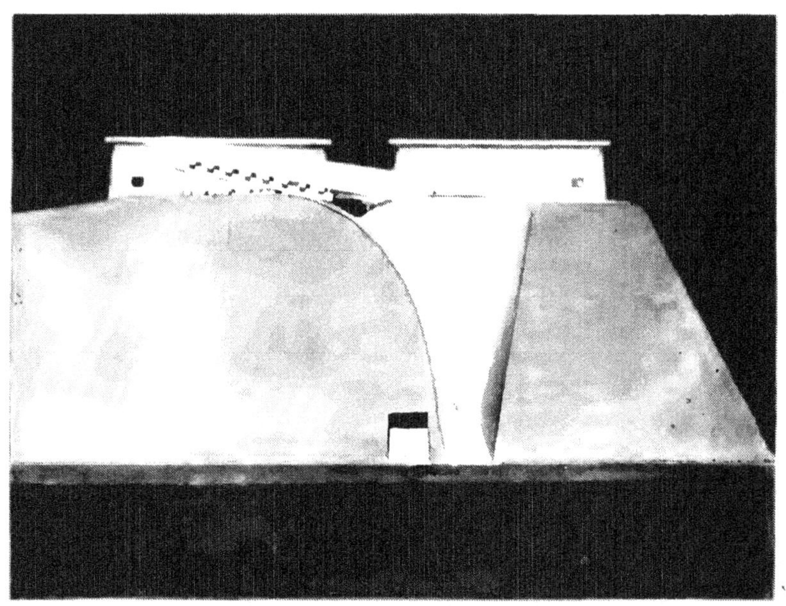

Fig. 30. OBELISK ENGAGING IN THE SAND; ALL THE LASHINGS ARE RELEASED.
(*Page* 71.)

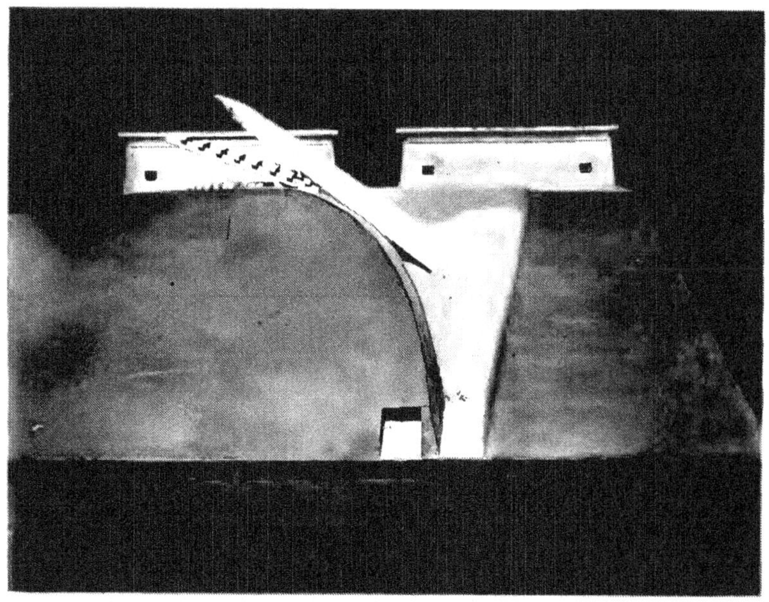

Fig. 31.—OBELISK HALF-WAY DOWN THE FUNNEL.
(*Page* 71.)

edge of the notch instead of on its own edge, which will thus be preserved from damage. Hatshepsôwet's obelisk, through missing the notch, split the corner B severely, which had to be rounded off to cover up the defect. Besides this, the notch had another function, which was to prevent the obelisk from twisting when it was pulled upright, and the Queen's obelisk—again through missing the notch—has twisted considerably, its position being CDEF instead of C'D'E'F' (fig. 25, p. 68). It is likely that part of the wall of the funnel had to be cut away to enable the obelisk to be pulled upright, though in any case I should imagine that enough space was left between the base of the obelisk and the funnel to enable men to get round and remove any stones, etc., which might have come down in the sand. It is seen, therefore, that the notch, although not an essential to the process of erection, is necessary for a perfect piece of work.

As soon as the obelisk had come down into its notch (fig. 32), men would enter through the gallery leading in from the end of the embankment, and clear every particle of sand from under the base, before it was pulled upright (fig. 33). Any tendency to rock after passing its dead-centre could be avoided by filling the space between the obelisk and the further wall of the funnel with coarse brushwood to act as a sort of cushion. The reason why I suppose that the sand was removed from the front gallery (which leads into the left side of the funnel) is that, if it were removed through the end gallery, there would be a far greater likelihood for the obelisk to jam against the opposite wall, since the flow of sand would be forwards rather than from under the obelisk.

An alternative possibility for the form of the funnel is that it had vertical walls in a transverse sense, the width being but very slightly greater than that of the base of the obelisk ; in other words, made so that the obelisk entered like a penny in the slot. By this means, full advantage would be taken of the weight of the sand above the obelisk, which would have the effect of bringing the base downward. I think, however, that the advantage gained would be discounted by the difficulty of controlling the descent by digging, etc., but it is a possibility which must be taken into serious consideration.

In the base of the now fallen obelisk of Tuthmôsis III, which stood before the pylons of Tuthmôsis I at Karnak, there are two rounded depressions near the centre. These may have been for inserting soft wooden blocks to act as shock-absorbers and to prevent the obelisk from tilting itself upright, prematurely, in its descent. The curious marks on the pedestal of the west obelisk of Luxor Temple may have fulfilled a similar purpose.

It is noteworthy, in the pedestals of the various obelisks, that their notches are not on the river side of the pedestals, even, as in the case of the obelisk which once stood before Pylon VII at Karnak, when the distance to the river was nearly 400 yards. To obtain sufficient height in the embankment, this obelisk had to be taken directly inland and brought back on an embankment which must have been constructed right over the Sacred Lake. Existing pylons prevented it from being brought to its pedestal parallel to the river, as was done in the case of the obelisks of Tuthmôsis I and III on the axis of the temple at Karnak. This is another hint that the embankment theory is correct.

Before we can say that the funnel theory is a possibility, we have to make sure that the largest obelisk known will not break owing to its great weight when supported at or pivoting round its centre of gravity or balancing-point. The non-technical reader will grasp this point better if he realises that a model obelisk like that shown in the photographs, which can be supported anywhere, and even leaned upon as well, without breaking, will not behave in the same way if it is magnified some 200 times, although the proportions are identical and the material the same. The strain due to its own weight is proportional to the linear dimensions of the monument. I will not give here the extremely wearisome calculation for the strain set up, but it is given in full in *The Aswan Obelisk*, and shows that even it could be supported anywhere without straining the granite to more than two-thirds what it can possibly stand. This is a narrow enough margin, and to endure this strain the granite would have to be flawless. Although the mathematics of the Egyptians was totally incapable of determining such stresses, they knew very well that such a long obelisk, if not perfectly sound, would inevitably break during the erecting process, if not long before. One, called Dhutiy (p. 106), mentions in his tomb inscription at Thebes that he erected two obelisks of 108 cubits in length, but unless the obelisks were much thicker than all known examples in proportion to their length, they would not have stood the strain of transport and erection.

The greater colossi, such as those of "Memnon" and the gigantic granite figure of Ramesses II in the Ramesseum, must have been erected in much the same manner as obelisks. The notches in the pedestals show them to have been brought in sideways, probably when they were merely roughed out. There must have been, of course, slight differences in the technique of the process, especially in the form of the funnel; the edges of the colossi, too, come flush with the edge of the pedestals with the notches well inside them. It seems likely that, in the case of colossi, the notch was filled with wood, on to which the monument came down; that is, the edge of the colossus was protected by the raised baulk of wood, held steady in the notch, instead of by the notch itself. This subject needs a good deal of further study.

One of the more surprising theories on the erecting process, which savours somewhat of Heath Robinson's mechanical studies, may be of interest. This is that put forward by Auguste Choisy in *L'Art de bâtir chez les Egyptiens*.

According to him the obelisk was raised by a series of weighted horizontal levers acting along its length, earth being banked under the obelisk at each heave, suitable supporting surfaces for the fulcra of the levers, in the form of masonry sides to the bank, being made, and heightened as the obelisk rose. Fig. 34, taken from his book, makes this clear.

His method of erecting is shown in figs. 35 and 36. He says: "Having arrived at a height *a*, let us pass, below it, cross-beams *c* and a pivot (tourillon) *n*. Now nothing prevents us from getting rid of the earth and constructing a *glissière*, or slide, *g*. Having made the slide, let us replace the removed earth by sand; let us remove the supports *c* and take away the sand. The obelisk, pivoting about *n*, will reach position *a*", and finally attain the vertical above its base *b*. It will be sufficient, to prevent it going too far, to reserve at *d* a buffer, and to hold back the top of the obelisk by head-ropes."

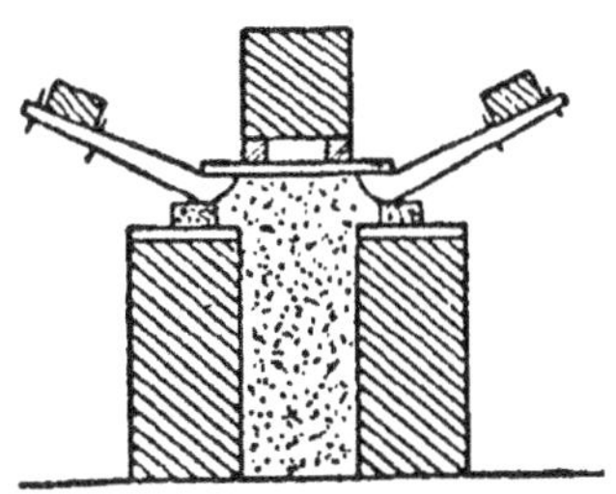

FIG. 34.—CHOISY'S SUGGESTION FOR RAISING OBELISKS.

He does not tell us what the *tourillon* is to be made of to stand the enormous strain, nor does he give any details as to the nature of the slide which would allow the point of the sled to slide over it and not jam hard. His attachment of the obelisk on the sled and the recess in the latter for holding back the obelisk are quite unsupported by any evidence. He goes on to say that the obelisk was lowered down on to its pedestal

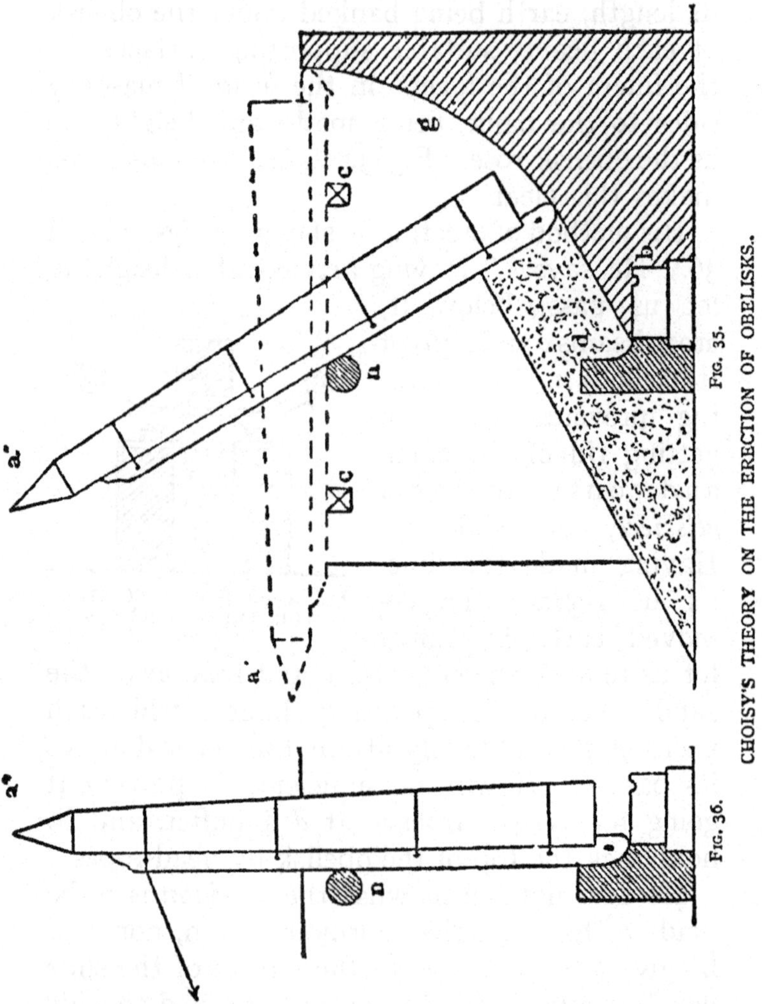

Fig. 35. Fig. 36.

CHOISY'S THEORY ON THE ERECTION OF OBELISKS.

by puncturing filled sand-bags which had been packed between it and the pedestal when in position *a‴*. His explanation of the notch is that it was to take a sausage-shaped bag, which was to be punctured last, after having removed the debris of the others. The mechanics of the method seem to me to be quite unsound, and the crushing of the inner edges of the pedestal-notches and the position of Hatshepsôwet's obelisk on its pedestal are not explainable by Choisy's theory.

It is rather difficult to say whether the Egyptians used scale models of obelisks to determine their weights and balancing-points, and to rehearse the erecting process. I am of opinion that they did; at any rate, there are quite a number of small obelisks known; one of Amenophis II has just been found at Aswan, which weighed under a ton. Apart from the determination of the bending stress (p. 75), the convenience of making use of models in this way cannot have escaped them. The final function of these small obelisks seems to have been to place them on either side of shrines, and especially of the Divine Boats. We have the description of the furniture provided for the sacred barge of the god Amûn in the time of Amenophis III. We are told (Breasted, *Ancient Records*, II, § 888):—

It was made very wide and large; there is no instance of the like being done. Its . . . is adorned with silver, wrought with gold throughout; the great shrine is of electrum, so that it fills the land with its brightness; its bows are as bright. They bear great crowns, and serpents twine along its two sides to protect them. Flagstaves, wrought with electrum, are set up before it, with two great obelisks between them; it is beautiful everywhere.

A model of a temple of the time of Seti I was found near Cairo, in which the base, which is of gritstone, shows the sockets in which the model pylons, colossi, obelisks and even the last pair of the avenue-sphinxes were fixed. Although this does not appear to have been an architect's working-model, having probably served some religious purpose in the temple like the tools and implements always found in temple foundation-deposits, it at least shows that the Egyptians were no strangers to making models of things other than tools, furniture and objects of art.

I had intended to devote a chapter to the polishing and engraving of obelisks after they were set up, but our knowledge of the engraving of the hard rocks is so vague that it can be summed up in a paragraph. The *details* of the processes, as given in the various works on the subject, are not clear to me—perhaps owing to my reprehensible habit of making experiments. The fundamental principles are, however, tolerably plain, and are summed up in Prof. Petrie's *Arts and Crafts in Ancient Egypt.* There is no doubt that the faces of the obelisks were dressed by the dolerite balls until they were as flat as possible, tests being made, as in engineering work to-day, by putting against them a portable flat plane smeared with red ochre and oil, or " ruddle " as the red lead and oil, now used for this purpose, is called. Prof. Petrie says that it was considered flat enough if the touches of red ochre from the plane were not separated by more than an inch, but I think he means this to refer to the sarcophagi and medium-sized monuments. In an obelisk the accuracy seems to have been far less (p. 37). The basis of the polishing and the engraving was most certainly emery stone and powder. There are indications that granite was cut with tubular drills and sometimes sawn, but we are more than doubtful how the emery was used. On page 72 of the work quoted, the situation is summed up as follows: "The difficult question is whether the material (emery) was used as loose powder, or was set in the metal tool as separate teeth. An actual example was found in the prehistoric Greek palace of Tiryns. The hard limestone there has been sawn, and I found a broken bit of the saw left in a cut. The copper blade had rusted away to green carbonate, and with it were some little blocks of emery about a sixteenth of an inch long, rectangular, and quite capable of being set, but far too large to act as a loose powder with a plain blade. On the Egyptian examples there are long grooves in the faces of the cuts of both saws and drills; and grooves may be made by working a loose powder. But, further, the groove certainly seems to run spirally round a core, which would show that it was cut by a single point. . . . The large hieroglyphs (p. 74) on hard stones were cut by copper blades fed with emery, and sawn along the outline by hand; the block between the cuts was broken out, and the floor of the sign was hammer-dressed and finally ground down with emery."

Before leaving the subject of the mechanical details connected with obelisks it may be of interest to inquire whether the Egyptians ever took them down. Pliny (p. 88) tells us that, under the Ptolemies, obelisks were moved, and we are very certain that the Romans and Byzantines did so on several occasions (p. 110). We have only one indication on this point, but it is of interest, since the inclusion of the word "obelisks" on a pylon not only answers the question, but makes us reconsider the usually accepted dating of an important building. The evidence is as follows: On the pylon of Amenophis III behind the Great Hypostyle Hall at Karnak, now known in the guide-books as Pylon III, the king, in an inscription on the east face, tells how wonderfully he decorated it. The inscription concludes:—"August . . . of electrum and obelisks. . . ." Now when Tutankhamûn, some 25 years after his death, celebrated the return to the worship of Amûn, he cut reliefs of the procession on the screen-walls of the great colonnade of the Temple of Luxor. He shows twice, in great detail, the pylon of Amenophis III, with its flagstaves and scenes, but there are no obelisks shown. During the Aten heresy all building work in Thebes was stopped in the temple of Amûn. The inference is that Amenophis III himself took them down. The only reason for him taking them down would be because he had the Hypostyle Hall, or at least the central colonnade, in his mind. This is far more likely than the supposition that Haremhab or Ramesses I put such a colossal piece of work in hand, as their building activities were small. Such a conception is quite in keeping, however, with the character of Amenophis III. The pillars are of typical XIXth dynasty work, so the king must have died almost as soon as the plan of the new building had been set out. The explanation that he took down the obelisks to put them in the temple of Monthu, north of the main temple, is unlikely, as the king would not take down his obelisks from the most important site in Upper Egypt and put them in a far less important place. Another indication that the Temple of Monthu was not their destination is that the pedestals of the obelisks there show that they were comparatively small; to my mind too small to have been those used before his pylon in the main temple. Where these obelisks actually went is rather a mystery, unless the king took them across the river, after having ordered a new pair for his great temple behind the Colossi of "Memnon," which we know was furnished with obelisks. It is generally admitted that the Grand Colonnade at Luxor, which was completed by Tutankhamûn and usurped by Haremhab, was commenced by Amenophis III as an addition to his own temple; it is therefore not unreasonable to suppose that he also began a similar building before his pylon at Karnak. Whether these additions were intended by him to be hypostyle halls or colonnades is uncertain; I think the latter is more probable, since Tutankhamûn, from the little we know of him, would not have done more than complete any building he found nearly finished. If he had found a hypostyle hall, the columns would all have been of one height in whatever state of completion the hall happened to be, since it appears to have been the Egyptian method to fill the building up with earth as the work became higher. The transformation of a hypostyle hall into a simple colonnade would have been a formidable undertaking. At Karnak, the history of the work appears to have been as follows: Haremhab and Ramesses I carried on with the plan of a colonnade left by Amenophis, and, before he died, Ramesses I was able to inscribe his name on one of the columns. When Seti I—a great building king—came to the throne, he changed the whole scheme, and developed the colonnade of Amenophis III into the Great Hypostyle Hall. All this speculation is raised by the inclusion, on a pylon, of the word "obelisks."

CHAPTER VII

SOME ANCIENT RECORDS

SOME idea as to the number of men employed on the transport of stone can be obtained from the following three accounts of expeditions.

King Menthuhotpe IV, of the XIth dynasty, sent an expedition to the Wady Hammâmmât to quarry stone for a large sarcophagus, and it is recorded that 10,000 men were sent out there. We are further told that it took 3,000 sailors from the Delta Provinces to remove the lid, which measured 13 feet 10 inches by 6 feet 5 inches by 3 feet 2½ inches deep, from the quarry to the river. The "sailors" were probably a pressed gang of the amphibious inhabitants of the Delta lakes. The expedition seems to have been fortunate, as we are told that not a man perished, not a trooper was missing, not an ass died, and not a workman was enfeebled (Breasted, *Ancient Records*, I, § 448).

In the reign of King Amenemhêt III, of the XIIth dynasty, an official, also called Amenemhêt, was sent to the same spot for 10 statues, each 8 feet 8 inches high. The personnel was made up as follows (Breasted, *Ancient Records*, I, § 710) :—

Necropolis soldiers	20
Sailors	30
Quarrymen	30
Troops	2,000

Under Ramesses IV a large expedition was again sent to the Wady Hammâmmât for monumental stone. It numbered 8,362 persons, and consisted of :—

High Priest of Amûn, Ramesses-nakht, Director of Works	1
Civil and military officers of rank	9
Subordinate officers	362
Trained artificers and artists	10
Quarrymen and stonecutters	130
Gendarmes	50
Slaves	2,000
Infantry	5,000
Men from Ayan	800
Dead (excluded from total)	900
	8,362

It will be seen from these figures that huge numbers of men were sent far afield for monuments much smaller than the Aswan obelisk. It seems to have been the custom to use troops on this unpleasant kind of fatigue. It might be observed by the facetiously-minded person that the present-day unpopularity of all recruiting measures in Egypt is but an inherited race-instinct. As there was always a garrison at Aswan, large numbers of men would be available at very short notice. Another point in the above list is the relatively small proportion of actual quarrymen and stonemasons. Since the rock in the Wady Hammâmmât was basalt—and very hard—it is more than probable that the extraction of the monuments was done by pounding, and that the quarrymen and stonemasons were only needed to direct the unskilled labourers and to perform the skilled work, such as making the wedge-slots when necessary and to examine the quality of the rock. How much finishing was done out in the desert we have no means of knowing.

The record of Queen Hatshepsôwet as to the length of time spent on the Karnak obelisks is given on pages 49 and 104.

In a papyrus known as the Papyrus Anastasi I, which is a kind of collection of model letters for scribes to copy, one scribe called Hori writes to another called Amenemôpe hinting that he is not up to his job. He says (Gardiner, *Egyptian Hieratic Texts*, § XIII) :—" An obelisk has been newly made . . . of 110 cubits (190 feet) ; its pedestal is 10 cubits (17½ feet) square, and the block of its base makes 7 cubits in every direction ; it goes in a slope (?) towards the summit (?) one cubit one finger, its pyramidion is one cubit in height, its point measuring two fingers. Combine them so as to make them into a list, that thou mayest appoint every man needed to drag it. . . ." Here the obelisk is extremely long, with a ridiculously short pyramidion, and the problem is an impossible one to solve for anyone who is not acquainted with the results of previous work in the quarry, and who is not familiar with the ground to be covered. The figures given are only sufficient to determine the weight of the obelisk. If such a problem was a typical one that scribes had to solve, the conclusion is that some kind of statistical record was kept in the archives of the various seats of learning to which the scribes had access. In other words, the experience of previous undertakings was at the disposal of the scribes.

Details of the transport of the winged bull at Nineveh are given on pages 56 and 57, and of the transport of the statue of Dhuthotpe on page 58.

Greek and Roman writers throw very little light on the transport and erection of large monuments except in giving dimensions of the blocks transported. Herodotus, in Book II, Chapter 175, tells us that King Amasis II brought a building of one stone from Elephantine which measured 34 feet 7 inches by 23 feet by 13 feet externally, and 30 feet 10 inches by 20 feet by 8 feet 4 inches internally, and that the 2,000 men appointed to convey it—who we are told were all pilots—took three whole years to perform their task.

Pliny, in his *Natural History*, Book XXXVI, Chapter 14, gives a slightly more valuable account of how King Ptolemy Philadelphus had an obelisk transported to Alexandria. He tells us that it was done by digging a canal from the Nile to the spot where the obelisk lay, passing below it, so that the obelisk was supported on either bank. Two large barges loaded with stones were unballasted below the obelisk which, rising, received its weight. This may well have been true, but it was not the way in which the Egyptians transported them, for there is no trace of a canal near the Aswan quarries.

The Egyptians, as it has already been remarked, have left us practically no information at all as to how they erected their obelisks. There is, however, a passage in the Anastasi Papyrus which refers to the erection of a colossus, and which is perhaps worth recording here, since it is fairly certain that the principle of the erection of the larger colossi was very similar to that of the erection of an obelisk (p. 76). The text gives :—" It is said to thee : Empty the *magazine that has been loaded with sand under the monument* of thy Lord, which has been brought from the Red Mountain. It makes 30 cubits stretched on the ground and 20 cubits in breadth . . . -ed with 100 chambers (?) filled with sand from the river bank. The . . . of its chambers have a breadth of 44 (?) cubits and a height of 50 cubits, all of them . . . in their . . . Thou art commanded to remove (overturn) it in six hours." Here, owing to errors in re-copying, and our slight knowledge of the technical terms mentioned, we are at a total loss as to the meaning of the second sentence.

In the same papyrus (§ XIII) there is a reference to an embankment which may well have been intended for the erection of an obelisk, as the problem immediately following it is that dealing with the transport of an obelisk, which has already been quoted. The scribe Hori puts the problem thus:—"There is a ramp to be made of 730 cubits (418 yards) with a breadth of 55 cubits (31·5 yards) consisting of 120 compartments (?) filled with reeds and beams having a height of 60 cubits (34·4 yards) at its summit. Its middle is 30 cubits (17·2 yards), its batter 15 cubits (8·6 yards), its base (?) 5 cubits (2·87 yards). The quantity of bricks for it is asked of the commander of the army. Behold its measurements are before thee; each one of its compartments is 30 cubits long and 7 cubits broad. . . ." Here, as before, the words "compartment" and "base" are of very doubtful meaning, and it is difficult to arrive at any definite idea on the construction of the ramp apart from its overall measurements. However one tries to arrange compartments in the ramp, an impossible situation follows, so we are compelled to believe that there is some error in the figures due to re-copying. It is likely that the compartments refer to the internal division of the ramp which, as it were, is a brick box, filled with earth for economy; on the other hand, the word may mean the externally visible sections or towers always found in very large brick walls. For full notes on these walls, see Somers Clarke, *Journal of Egyptian Archæology*, Vol. VII, p. 77.

The only account of the erection of an obelisk

by the Egyptians is that given by Pliny, which cannot fail to appeal to those who have had the fortune (?) to fall into the hands of an Egyptian dragoman. He must have livened up the visitors even in those days. Pliny was told that King "Rhamsesis," when an obelisk was being put up, feared that the machinery employed would not be strong enough, so he had his own son tied to the summit in order to make the workmen more careful. If this "Rhamsesis" was Ramesses II, the loss of a son would not have been vital, as he is known to have had over a hundred, to say nothing of several score daughters!

CHAPTER VIII

A HISTORY OF CERTAIN OBELISKS AND THEIR ARCHITECTS

ALTHOUGH the ancient records and other notes given in this chapter are somewhat of a digression from the main subject of the book—the mechanical problems connected with obelisks—they are of interest, since they give us glimpses, not only of the curious history of some of the better-known obelisks, but of the lives and characters of the men who were responsible for their quarrying and erection. Fortunately, the tombs of most of the obelisk-architects are known to us, since their efforts on behalf of their kings were usually rewarded by the present of a tomb in the most fashionable part of the Theban necropolis, and of a statue in the temple. Though they were debarred from putting the ancient version of " So-and-so fecit " on their obelisks, they made up for it in their tombs by recording with pride that they had put up obelisks for the king, and they become garrulous in recounting what good workmen they were, and how well they treated their subordinates, specially emphasising the rewards they received and the titles and decorations granted to them. But they say nothing as to how they did their job ; it sufficed that it was done. This omission—so strange to our minds—

seems to me to be due to the fact that there was only one method of putting up an obelisk, which was well known. It seems more than likely, however, that full details of each piece of work were kept for the information and guidance of scribes.

The obelisk of Tuthmôsis I, shown in the frontispiece, which, with its now fallen fellow, stood before his pylon (No. IV at Karnak), was erected by a noble called Ineni, who also constructed the pylon and court of Osirid figures behind it, and excavated the King's tomb in the royal valley. His active life began under Amenophis I (see Appendix II) and continued into the second reign of Tuthmôsis III, when in co-regency with Queen Hatshepsôwet. The times in which he lived were prosperous but stormy, especially during the latter end of his career, when the relations between Tuthmôsis III and the Queen were more than strained. Perhaps it is fortunate that he died before the open rupture took place, or he might have shared, with Sennemût and others of the Queen's party, the hatred of Tuthmôsis III when at length he ruled alone. Ineni's sympathies clearly lay with Hatshepsôwet. In his tomb (No. 81 at Thebes) he gives quite an entertaining account of his life. His titles were: Pasha, Count, Chief of all the Works in Karnak, Controller of the Double-houses of Silver and of Gold, Sealer of all Contracts in the House of Amûn, and Excellency in Charge of the Double-Granary. The beginning of his tomb-inscription is missing, but he appears to have been foreman on the work of Amenophis I's gate to the south of the Karnak temple and of his mortuary temple on the west side. Ineni tells us (*cf.* Breasted, *Ancient Records*, II, § 45) :—

. . . . its doors were erected of copper made in one sheet ; parts of them were of electrum. I inspected that which His Majesty made . . . (of) bronze, Asiatic copper—collars, vessels and necklaces. I was foreman of every work ; all offices were under my command. . . . Inspection was made for me—I was the reckoner.

Describing the death of the king, he says :—

His Majesty, having spent his life in happiness and the years in peace, went forth to heaven. He joined the Sun ; he associated with Him and went forth.

Under Tuthmôsis I, Ineni obtained the superintendence of the king's building projects, and he begins the next part of his story by impressing on the reader how thoroughly Egypt and Nubia were under his authority. After recording the new king's kindness to him, he says :—

I inspected the great monuments which he made [a great hall] ; with great pylons on either side of it made of fine Ayan limestone. August flagstaves were erected at the double façade of the temple, of new fir-trees of the best of the Terraces (Lebanon ?), whose tips were of electrum (silver-gold alloy). . . . I inspected the putting-up of the great doorway called : Amûn-Mighty-in-Wealth ; its huge door was of Asiatic copper, whereon was the Divine Shadow, inlaid with gold. I inspected the erection of two obelisks . . . and built the " august " boat of 120 cubits (206·6 feet) in length and 40 cubits (68·86 feet) in breadth for transporting these obelisks. They came in peace safety and prosperity, and landed at Karnak. . . . Its track (?) was laid with every pleasant wood. I inspected the excavations of the cliff-tomb of His Majesty—no one seeing, no one hearing— . . . I made fields of clay for plastering the tombs of the Necropolis. I was obliged to do a job which the ancestors had not had done. . . .

After again assuring us that he was really a first-class engineer, and immensely popular into the bargain, he records the death of the king, saying that he "rested from life, going forth to heaven, having completed his years in gladness of heart."

Under Tuthmôsis II, Ineni seems not to have engaged in any work of importance, and he says that he is getting old; but he records with pride that he was supplied with food from the king's own table until Tuthmôsis II also died, or, as Ineni puts it, "mingled with the gods."

During the cat-and-dog life of Hatshepsôwet and Tuthmôsis III, the old courtier had retired from all active work, but seems to have been a keen observer of the state of the court. On the accession of the king and queen he observes:

His (Tuthmôsis II's) son stood in his place as King of Egypt, having become ruler in the place of him who begat him. His sister, the Divine Consort, settled the affairs of Egypt according to her ideas. . . .

The ending of Ineni's inscription does not err on the side of modesty. He concludes thus:—

I became great beyond words; I will tell you about it, ye people; listen and do the good that I did—just like me. I continued powerful in peace and met with no misfortune; my years were spent in gladness. I was neither a traitor nor a sneak, and I did no wrong whatever. I was foreman of the foremen, and did not fail. . . . I never hesitated, but always obeyed superior orders . . . and I never blasphemed sacred things.

Such was the career of Ineni, whose inscription, when analysed, is of very great importance historically. If he handled oriental labour for some forty years without blaspheming it was not the least of his achievements.

The inscriptions on this obelisk are like those of most other obelisks, and are merely the elaborate titulary of the king and the fact of the dedication to the god. They have no general interest beyond giving the reign under which it was erected. Here the middle columns only are contemporary, the side ones being titles and encomiums added by Ramesses IV and VI some four centuries later. As an example of a dedication formula, the east and west sides may be translated as follows, the north and south sides being only titles :—

(East) Horus; Mighty Bull, beloved of Truth; King of Upper and Lower Egypt; Favourite of the Two Goddesses; Shining with the Serpent Diadem, great in strength; Okheperkerê Setepnerê; Golden Horus; Beautiful in Years, who makes hearts to live; Bodily son of Rê, Tuthmôsis (I), Shining in Beauty.

He made it as his monument to his father Amûn, Lord of Thebes, Presider over Karnak, that he may be given life, like Rê, eternally.

(West) Horus; Mighty Bull, beloved of Truth, King of Upper and Lower Egypt, Okheperkerê, Setep-Amûn.

He made it as his monument to his father Amen-Rê, Chief of Egypt, erecting for him two great obelisks at the double-façade of the temple. The pyramidions are of [electrum]. . . .

When the fragments of the companion obelisk were discovered, it was found that they were inscribed, not by Tuthmôsis I, but by Tuthmôsis III. Ineni is quite clear about his having erected *two* obelisks before the pylons. From this we deduce that after the second obelisk had been erected, but before it was inscribed, Tuthmôsis I died. We are therefore driven to one of two conclusions: either that the obelisk remained uninscribed for some twenty-three years until Tuthmôsis III held the throne, being neither usurped by Tuthmôsis II nor Hatshepsôwet—which is extremely improbable—or that Tuthmôsis III reigned for a certain period before Tuthmôsis II! Strange as this may seem, it is borne out by quite a large amount of evidence. The probable order of the Tuthmosids was somewhat as follows:—

(1) Tuthmôsis I either abdicates or is suppressed.

(2) Tuthmôsis III reigns alone, possibly as a child, protected by a strong party.

(3) Hatshepsôwet's party forces her upon Tuthmôsis III as co-regent; he may have acquiesced since, by marrying the heiress, he would make his title secure.

(4) After Tuthmôsis III had been on the throne some six years in all, Tuthmôsis I and II

seize the throne, but are unable to make Tuthmôsis III relinquish his claims on it.

(5) Tuthmôsis I dies, and a co-regency of Tuthmôsis II and III follows, which lasts till Tuthmôsis II's death two years later.

(6) Hatshepsôwet and Tuthmôsis III rule together for twelve years, until the former either dies or is forced to retire.

(7) Tuthmôsis III rules alone, and cuts out the names of the queen and her supporters wherever he finds them.

Even this complicated sequence does not absolutely explain all the observed facts, and it is still a matter of conjecture how such a state of affairs arose. The successors of these rulers—who seem to have thrived in spite of the most grotesque in-breeding—have, it seems, treated the matter as a private affair and hushed it up, recording the order of each according to the period in which he reigned longest, namely, Tuthmôsis I, Tuthmôsis II and Tuthmôsis III. Hatshepsôwet is omitted as, though her husband ruled through her, she could not by custom reign alone.

The above brief historical précis has been included to show how a simple dedicatory inscription may give the key to a most extraordinary political situation, and to enable the reader better to understand the conditions under which the next four architects performed their work.

Hatshepsôwet's standing obelisk at Karnak—the second largest survivor—was erected by

Sennemût, who was perhaps the staunchest supporter of the queen against Tuthmôsis III. Not only did he play an important part in her expedition to Punt (Somaliland), but he was her chief architect at Karnak, Luxor, Dêr El-Bahari and Hermonthis (Armant). So great a favourite was he with the queen that he, together with a noble called Ahmôse-pen-Nekh-beyet, shared between them the rearing of her daughter, the heiress, Nefrurê. A further mark of the royal favour was that his statues were presented to him by the queen and Tuthmôsis III—the latter, perhaps, under compulsion—to be set up in the temple of Karnak. One of the statues of Sennemût holding Nefrurê is shown in fig. 37. He was even included and mentioned by name in the adoration-scene of the south colonnade at Dêr El-Bahari—a most unusual honour. Hatshepsôwet's power seemed to rest on Sennemût and two other nobles called Nehsi ("The Sudanese") and Dhutiy, the last being also an expert in obelisks. Their figures are chiselled out at Dêr El-Bahari and their tombs, especially that of Sennemût (No. 71 at Thebes), were mutilated by Tuthmôsis III after the fall of the queen. In contrast to Sennemût, Puimrê, yet another obelisk-maker, continued to work as energetically for Tuthmôsis III in later years as for Hatshepsôwet, for whom he had made an ebony shrine. Can it be that here we have an ancient "Vicar of Bray"? Sennemût, at any rate, preferred to fall with his queen.

Sennemût's tomb is almost completely

destroyed, but his statues give the details of the work he did. Though Tuthmôsis III cut out his name, he left the inscription intact. It is from here that we learn that his titles were Pasha, Count, Royal Seal-bearer, Sole Companion, Chief Steward of Amûn, Chief of the Prophets of Monthu in Armant, Controller of the Fields, Gardens and Cattle of Amûn, Chief Steward of the King and Chief of the Peasant-serfs. Though Hepusonb (tomb No. 81) was Vizier, there is no doubt that Sennemût was the power behind the throne. The inscriptions on his statues are of the usual formal character and are hardly worth giving at length. On one he says, after recording the favour of the "King," as Hatshepsôwet preferred to be called :—

I was the greatest of the great in the whole land; one who had audience alone in the Privy Council. I was the real favourite of the King. . . . I was foreman of the foremen ; superior of the great. . . . I was one to whom the affairs of Egypt were reported. That which the South and North contributed was sealed by me ; the labour of all countries was under my charge.

Then follows an appeal to all living men upon earth, who see his statue, to say the usual prayer for his *ka* or double, and the inscription concludes :—

I was a noble who was obeyed ; moreover, I had access to all the writings of the prophets ; there was nothing which I did not know concerning what had happened since the beginning.

He shows his knowledge of the classics by

Fig. 37.—STATUE OF SENNEMÛT, ARCHITECT OF HATSHEPSÔWET'S OBELISKS, HOLDING HER DAUGHTER NEFRURÊ, TO WHOM HE WAS TUTOR.

quoting an archaic formula which had long fallen into disuse.

His second statue, which is that of the illustration on page 100, has a more condensed inscription. In it he refers to his tutorship, and says how he " entered into all the wonderful plans of the Mistress of Egypt." Here, curiously enough, he says that his engineering appointment was due to " Him," although the feminine pronoun is maintained elsewhere in the inscription for Hatshepsôwet. Possibly this statue was presented when his relations with Tuthmôsis III were still fairly amicable.

We know nothing of Sennemût's parents except their names, which were Ramôse and Henûfer. His brother Senmen, however, was a very influential and powerful noble, and his tomb was also wrecked by Tuthmôsis III.

Sennemût has left an inscription on the rocks at Aswan where he appears adoring the queen. After giving her titles and his own, he records :—

> . . . Sennemût came in order to conduct the work of two great obelisks [on the feast of] A-Myriad-of-Years. It took place according to that which was commanded—everything was done—because of the fame of Her Majesty.

The vertical inscriptions on the great obelisk of Hatshepsôwet at Karnak are merely titles and laudatory phrases, and give no information at all of the character of the queen or the history of her times. The south, west and north sides give the elaborate titulary, and express the love that the god Amen-Rê bore her. At the end of the text on the east face she says :—

She repeated the action of her father, Tuthmôsis (I), in erecting obelisks, so that her name might also live for ever.

The inscriptions round the base of the standing obelisk are considerably more important, and are now considered to be the finest examples of the language of the period. The following is a translation :—

(South side) May the Horus (fem.) live . . . (the full titulary follows) . . . daughter of Amen-Rê, his favourite, his only one, who exists through him, the splendid part of the All-Lord, whose beauty the Spirits of Heliopolis fashioned ; who has taken the land like "The Begetter," whom he has created to wear his Diadem, who exists like Khepri (the god of the Rising Sun) who shines with crowns like "Him-of-the-Horizon" ; the pure egg, the excellent seed, whom the two Sorceresses (Isis and Nephthys) reared, whom Amûn himself caused to appear upon his throne in Armant, whom he chose to protect Egypt to defend the people ; the Horus, avenger of her father (Osiris), the eldest daughter of the "Bull-of-his-Mother" (a sun-god), whom Rê begat to make for himself excellent seed upon earth for the well-being of the people ; his living image, King of Upper and Lower Egypt, Makerê (Hatshepsôwet's throne-name), the "electrum" of kings.

She made them as her monument to her father Amûn, Lord of Thebes, Presider over Karnak, making for him two great obelisks of enduring granite from the south ; their summits are of electrum of the best of every country, and are seen on both sides of the river. Their rays flood the Two Lands when the sun rises between them as he dawns in the horizon of heaven.

I have done this from a loving heart for my father Amûn, I have entered into his scheme for his first jubilee; I was wise by his excellent spirit and forgot nothing of that which he exacted. (West side.) My Majesty knows that he is divine.

[1]I did it under his command: it was he who led me.
I conceived no works without his doing: it was he who gave me directions.
I slept not because of his temple: I erred not from that which he commanded.
My heart was wise before my father: I entered into the affairs of his heart.
I turned not my back on the City of The All-Lord: but turned to it the face.

I know that Karnak is the horizon upon earth, the August Ascent of the Beginning, the Sacred Eye of the All-Lord, the place of his heart, which wears his beauty, and encompasses those who follow him.

Thus saith the King: "I have set it before the people who shall be in after ages, and whose hearts shall consider this monument which I made for my father (an obscure phrase follows). . . . I sat in the palace, I remembered him who fashioned me; my heart led me to make for him two obelisks of electrum whose points mingled with heaven, in the august colonnade between the two great pylons of the King, the Mighty Bull, King of Upper and Lower Egypt, Okheperkerê (Tuthmôsis I) the deceased Horus. . . ."

O ye people (north side) who shall see my monument

[1] The phrasing of these five lines, it will be noticed, bears a striking resemblance to that of the Psalms.

in after years, those who shall speak of that which I have made beware lest ye say, "I know not, I know not why this was done—a mountain fashioned entirely from gold as if it were an everyday occurrence." [1]I swear, as Rê loves me, as my father Amûn favours me, as my nostrils are filled with life, as I wear the White Crown, as I appear in the Red Crown, as Horus and Set have united their halves in me, as I rule this land like the Son of Isis (*i.e.*, Horus), as I have become strong like the Son of Nût (Osiris), as Rê sets in the Boat of the Evening, and as He rises in the Boat of the Morning, as He joins his two Mothers (Isis and Nephthys—a confusion of the myths of Rê and Osiris) in the Divine Boat, as Heaven abides, as that which He made endures, as I shall be unto eternity like an Imperishable Star, as I shall go down into the west like Atûm (the god of the Setting Sun), so surely these two great obelisks, which My Majesty hath wrought with electrum for my father Amûn, that my name may abide in this temple eternally, are of one block of enduring granite without seam or joining. . . . My Majesty exacted work on them from the (regnal) year 15, the first of the sixth month (of the absolute year) until the year 16, the last of the twelfth month, making seven months of exaction in the mountain.

(East side) I did it for him in fidelity of heart, as a king to a god. It was my desire to make them for him, gilded with electrum. . . . I thought how people would say that my mouth was excellent because of that which came from it, for I did not turn back from what I had said. Hear ye! I gave for them of the finest electrum, which I had measured by the *heket*

[1] Although previously she had said that the tip was of electrum, it looks as if it was completely overlaid. This is perhaps why she swears so solemnly that they are of one piece, as the overlaying might well conceal a joint.

(5 litres, or just over a gallon) like sacks of grain. In quantity, My Majesty gave more than all Egypt had ever seen. The ignorant, like the wise, knoweth it.

Let not him who shall hear this say that what I have said is a lie, but rather let him say: " How like her it is who is truthful in the sight of her father! "

The God knew it in me, Amen-Rê, Lord of Thebes. He caused that I should reign over the Black and the Red land as a reward therefor. I have no enemy in any land; all countries are my subjects. He has made my boundary to the end of heaven; the circuit of the Sun has laboured for me . . . (an obscure phrase follows). . . . I am in truth his daughter who glorifies him. . . . Life, stability and satisfaction be upon the Horus Throne of the Living, like Rê, eternally!

At some period in the history of this obelisk, masonry was built all round it right up to the roof of the hall. This looks like the work of Tuthmôsis III, as the queen would never have covered up her inscription in this way. The difficulty is that the side scenes (see frontispiece) are unfinished, only reaching from the top to about half-way down the obelisk. An accurate knowledge of the Tuthmosid succession is necessary before the history of the obelisk can be fully understood. Another curious point is that the shaft of the fallen obelisk had been usurped by Tuthmôsis III, while in the standing obelisk the queen's name is untouched. In the pedestal inscription of the fallen obelisk, which is in fragments, the queen records that her kingdom reached Punt on the south, the Asiatic marshes on the east, and the legendary mountains of Manu on the west. Her northern boundary is no longer legible. She also recounts on it the wonderful tribute which was remitted to Egypt in her reign.

Another obelisk-architect under this queen was one Dhutiy, whose tomb (No. 11 at Thebes) has been mutilated by Tuthmôsis III. Among his many titles were Director of Works and Controller of the Double-houses of Silver and Gold. The great work by which he is known is the systematic recording of the treasures from the Punt expedition, and he appears—busily taking notes—in the reliefs in the temple of Dêr El-Bahari. As has been remarked, he was openly of the queen's party, and suffered in consequence. In addition to his recording work, he appears to have made gateways, shrines, thrones and small furniture for the temple of Karnak, and erected two great obelisks of 108 cubits (186 feet) high. We have no idea at all as to where these obelisks were placed ; further, it seems that such a high obelisk could not withstand its own weight during its transport and erection (p. 76), unless it was vastly thicker proportionately than all others, so it has been suggested that the length given is the total length of the pair when placed butt to butt on the giant barge. It is more likely that the figure is an error in transcription from the cursive notes from which the tomb-inscriptions were copied.

Puimrê, whose name has already been mentioned in connection with Sennemût, although he had done certain pieces of work for Queen

Hatshepsôwet, managed to retain the favour of Tuthmôsis III when he reigned alone. In his tomb (No. 39 at Thebes, lately restored) he states that he erected two obelisks for Tuthmôsis III at Karnak. By a process of elimination, it is likely that they were those which stood before Pylon VII at Karnak. Judging from the base measurements of the eastern fragment, they must have stood between 94 and 115 feet high, that is, higher than the great obelisk of Hatshepsôwet at Karnak, and only equalled by the Lateran obelisk at Rome (pages 30 and 108). The fragments of the companion obelisk have just been unearthed by the Antiquities Department and the foundations of the western pedestal exposed. Puimrê's inscriptions are of little interest. He tells us that he put up the obelisks (though he gives no measurements), that he made a limestone building and an ebony shrine, and that he recorded the tribute brought in from Watet-Hôr, probably a frontier on the Asiatic side of the Delta. His titles were Pasha, Count, Sole Companion, Royal Seal-Bearer and Divine Father. A statue of him was found during the excavations in the temple of Mût at Karnak.

The obelisks of Tuthmôsis III, which were placed before the two which Ineni had erected for Tuthmôsis I, thus forming a compact little group of four, seem to have been the work of Menkheperra-sonb, a name meaning something like "Here's to Tuthmôsis III!" These are shown being presented to Amûn on a relief by the side of the sanctuary of Karnak, of which a photograph is given in fig. 38, as the inscriptions here tally almost exactly with those still visible on the picture of the obelisk in his tomb (No. 86 at Thebes) and with the fragments of those lying between Pylons III and IV. His father appears to have been the powerful vizier Rekhmirê (tomb No. 100). His statue, too, has been found at Karnak. He was, among others, Controller of the Silver House and the Gold House, High Priest of Amûn, and Director General of Craftsmen. In his tomb, he says that he made two shrines—one of a single block of granite—and a colonnade. His work in connection with obelisks is recorded as follows :—

> I inspected when His Majesty erected obelisks and numerous flagstaves for his father Amûn. I pleased His Majesty while conducting the work on his monuments.

The largest standing obelisk known is that which now stands in front of the church of S. Giovanni in Laterno at Rome (for dimensions see p. 30). We are not certain whether it was erected by Puimrê, Menkheperra-sonb or another. It was made for Tuthmôsis III, but he appears to have died after it had reached its site and before it was erected. His grandson, Tuthmôsis IV, piously engraved and erected it before Pylon VIII at Karnak. It never had a fellow, and it is expressly stated that it was the first case of a single obelisk being erected. Tuthmôsis IV put it up in his grandfather's name, adding his own account of its history on the side

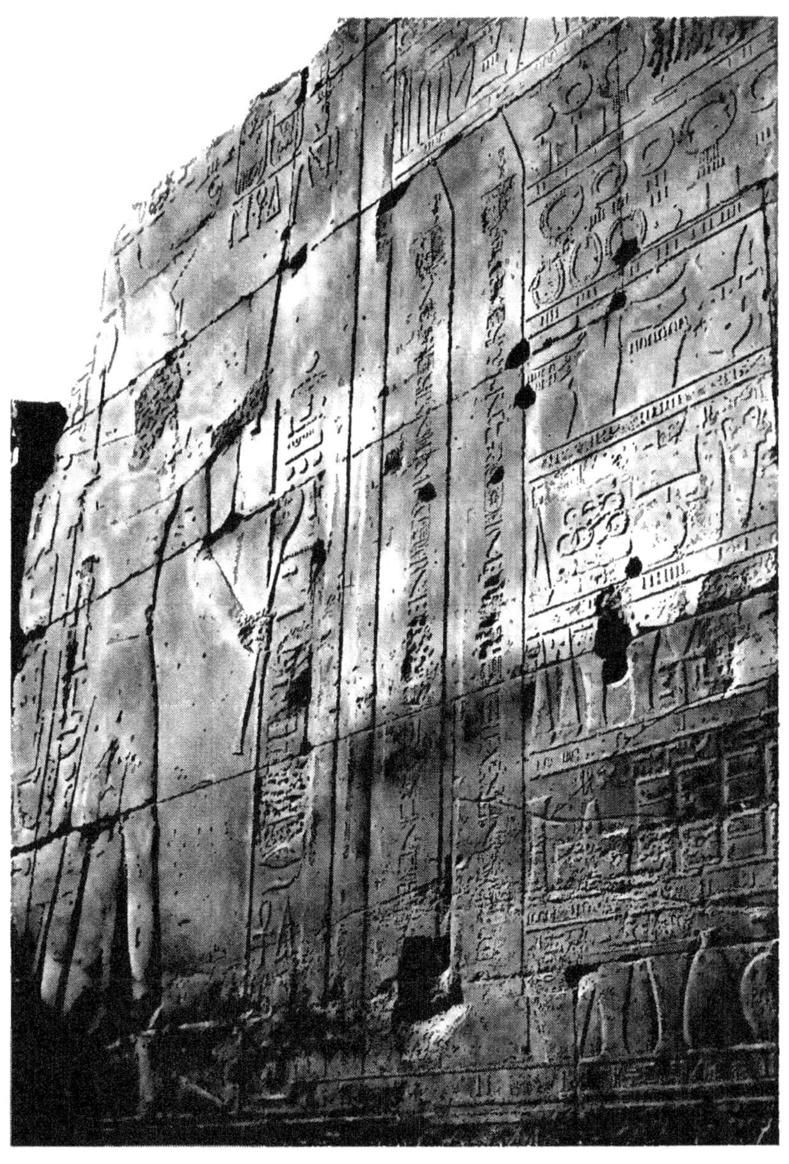

Fig. 38.—King Tuthmôsis III presents obelisks, flagstaves and booty from Palestine to the god Amen-Rê, Karnak.

columns of the shaft. Since the inscriptions are chiefly titles and encomiums, it will suffice to give the relevant portions which refer to its history. In the centre inscription on the south side we read :—

> Tuthmôsis (III) made it as his monument to his father Amen-Rê, Lord of Thebes, erecting for him a single obelisk in the forecourt of the temple over against Karnak, as a first instance of erecting a single obelisk in Thebes. . . .

Tuthmôsis IV gives the previous history on the left column of the south side. After giving his titles, etc., he says :—

> Tuthmôsis (IV). It was His Majesty who beautified the enormous single obelisk, which was one his father (*i.e.*, ancestor) . . . Tuthmôsis III had brought, after His Majesty had found this obelisk lying on its side, having passed 35 years in the hands of the craftsmen on the south side of Karnak. My father commanded that I should erect it for him, I, his son, his saviour.

Tuthmôsis IV goes on, with pride, to say that he engraved it with the name of his father. To our eyes it was his bounden duty, but it is certain that very few kings, except perhaps Seti I, would have done it.

The next thing we hear of this obelisk is its transport from Thebes to Alexandria in A.D. 330 under the reign of Constantine the Great, who intended to send it to Byzantium. About A.D. 357 his son Constantius took it to Rome, and set it up in the Circus Maximus. In 1587 it was discovered there broken in three pieces and was set up at its present site by Domenico Fontana in

1588. Whether it was removed from Egypt in a complete state or broken as it is now we have no means of knowing.

The great obelisk at Constantinople was taken from Thebes to Alexandria, it is believed, by Constantine the Great (A.D. 306–337), and there is a record that the Emperor Julian (A.D. 360–363) addressed a letter to the people of Alexandria urging them to forward the shaft to its destination and promising them a colossal statue of himself in return. It was erected in Constantinople by the Emperor Theodosius about A.D. 390. It originally stood in Karnak, and may well have been the work of Menkheperra-sonb. The bottom of the shaft is missing, so that it does not stand at its original height. Some have supposed that it was the top part of the 108-cubit obelisks recorded by Dhutiy (p. 106), but those were of the time of Hatshepsôwet, and this is clearly of Tuthmôsis III. It may be the upper part of one of those which stood between Pylons III and IV. Its inscriptions are without interest.

The "Cleopatra's Needles" at London and New York originally formed a pair in the temple of Heliopolis, and were removed to Alexandria in 13–12 B.C. by the Athenian (?) architect Pontius. One (now in London) apparently fell from its pedestal early in the fourteenth century. The only explanation I can give as to how it escaped breaking is that there was a considerable accumulation of sand around the base and in its neighbourhood which let it down gently. The inscriptions on both these obelisks are only titles and laudatory phrases and have no interest at all. They were erected by Tuthmôsis III and spoilt by the additions, in side columns, of the titles of Ramesses II. Their original architect is unknown. Pontius has, however, left us a brief inscription on the bronze cramps—shaped like crabs—which he inserted at each broken corner to give it additional support. These inscriptions in Greek and Latin read (according to Breasted) :—

Ŀ IH ΚΑΙΣΑΡΣ	ANNO XVIII CÆSARIS
ΒΑΡΒΑΡΟΣ ΑΝΕΘΗΚΕ	BARBARVS PRÆF
ΑΡΧΙΤΕΚΤΟΝ ΟΥΝΤΟΣ	ÆGYPTI POSVIT
ΠΟΝΤΙΟΥ	ARCHITECTANTE PONTIO

The history of their erections in New York and London is given on pages 117 and 121.

The Arab writer ‘Abd El-Latîf, in about A.D. 1190, when he visited Heliopolis, saw two great obelisks there, one standing and the other lying broken. Less than three centuries earlier both are reported to have been standing, adorned with their copper caps. For many centuries the second obelisk has been missing, the only one remaining being that of Senusret I, of which a photograph is shown in fig. 2, p. 18. While I was excavating there for the British School of Archæology in 1912, under Prof. Flinders Petrie, we found fragments of the second obelisk quite close to it under the cultivation. The second obelisk was not of the XIIth dynasty, but of Tuthmôsis III. These fragments have been arranged round the pedestal of the standing obelisk. (See Petrie, *Heliopolis, Kafr Ammar and Shurafa.*) Gorringe, in his *Egyptian Obelisks,* gives all the accounts of mediæval authors on the subject of the obelisks of Heliopolis.

During the XIXth dynasty our records about obelisks and their architects are fewer, though we know that many of them were erected. That in front of the Temple of Luxor, shown in fig. 39, whose fellow is now in the Place de la Concorde, Paris, was erected by a man called Beknekhonsu, whose tomb (No. 35 at Thebes) and whose statue, now at the Glyptothek, Munich, give us a great deal of information about his career. His autobiography is so clear that it can be given almost verbatim :—

The Pasha, Count, High Priest of Amûn, Beknekhonsu says : I was a truthful witness, profitable to his lord, extolling the instruction of his god . . . and performing the ceremonies in his temple. I was Chief Overseer of Works in the House of Amûn, satisfying the excellent heart of his lord.

O all ye people, take heed in your hearts ; ye who are on earth who shall come after me through millions and millions of years. . . . I will inform you of my character while I was on earth, in every office which I administered since my birth.

I passed four years as an infant.
I passed 12 years as a youth, being chief of the training stable of King Menmirê (Seti I).
I acted as priest of Amûn for 4 years.
I acted as Divine Father for 12 years.
I acted as third prophet of Amûn for 15 years.
I acted second prophet of Amûn for 12 years.

He favoured me and distinguished me because of my

Fig. 39.—OBELISK OF RAMESSES II, TEMPLE OF LUXOR.
(Its fellow is now at the Place de la Concorde, Paris.)

FIG. 40.—CONTEMPORARY SCULPTURE OF PYLON OF RAMESSES II IN THE TEMPLE OF LUXOR, SHOWING OBELISKS, FLAGSTAVES AND COLOSSI.
(*Page* 113.)

rare talent, and appointed me High Priest of Amûn for 27 years.

I was a good father to my serf-labourers, training their classes, giving a hand to him who was in trouble and preserving alive him who had met with misfortune. . . . I was Chief Overseer of Works in Thebes for his (Seti's) son, Ramesses (II), who made monuments for his father Amûn, who had placed him on the throne.

I made for him a temple called : Ramesses-Meriamûn-is-a-Hearer-of-Petitions, at the upper portal of the House of Amûn. I erected obelisks of granite therein, whose beauty approached heaven. A stone wall was before it over against Thebes. I made very great doors of electrum. . . . I hewed very great flagstaves and I erected them in the august forecourt before the temple.

A contemporary sculpture of the pylon, with its obelisks and flagstaves, is shown in fig. 40. Beknekhonsu concludes :—

I made great barges . . . for Amûn, Mût and Khonsu (the Theban triad) ; I, the Pasha and High Priest of Amûn, Beknekhonsu.

An account of the removal in modern times of the missing obelisk is given on page 116. It is a curious fact that the two were not exactly of the same height.

It must not be imagined that obelisks were made almost exclusively in the XVIIIth and XIXth dynasties. In Rome and elsewhe e there are obelisks and fragments of obelisks of many other kings, including Psammetikhos, Hophra, and even the Roman emperors Hadrian and Domitian.

CHAPTER IX

REMOVALS OF OBELISKS IN MODERN TIMES

ALTHOUGH the removals of obelisks from Egypt in recent times give us very little information which might help us to understand the methods of the ancients, a brief account of them is of interest if only for the contrast; it makes us appreciate the work of the Egyptians the more, especially when we bear in mind that every method used in modern days for the lowering and erection of an obelisk—which has never exceeded 331 tons in weight—always taxed the strength of the tackle to the utmost; in each case it was only just strong enough. Every modern removal has been a nine days' wonder, and a ponderous tome has appeared about it, yet the Egyptians, we know for a fact, set up obelisks of over 550 tons, and—if we are to believe their records—of more than 800 tons, without troubling to put on record how they did it.

The obelisks which we will deal with here are now known as the Vatican, the Paris, the London and the New York obelisks. The countries of the last two both claim their own to be the one and original "Cleopatra's Needle," though why they should be so keen on this title I cannot imagine, since they were both made by Tuthmôsis III some 14 centuries earlier.

The Vatican obelisk had been taken from Egypt in Roman times, and it was moved in A.D. 1586 by Domenico Fontana from the Circus of Nero at Rome to the Piazza di San Pietro, where it now stands, incongruously decorated —like most of the other obelisks in Italy—with a brazen cross. The removal was performed by order of Pope Sixtus V. The method used was the heroic one of lifting it bodily by systems of pulleys actuated by a large number of capstans. The pulleys were slung from a gigantic tower of wood, popularly known as "Fontana's Castle," which was made of compound wooden baulks over a yard square in section. The pulleys were attached to the obelisk at four points along its length, the inscriptions being protected by matting and planks. The obelisk was first raised sufficiently high, being wedged at the same time from below, to enable a "cradle," or platform on rollers, to be introduced underneath it. It was then lowered on to the cradle and pulled to its new site, first down an inclined plane and thence on level ground. The erecting was performed in exactly the reverse manner to the lowering. The whole story, as translated by Lebas in his *L'Obélisque de Louxor*, is distinctly diverting, and I cannot resist giving two extracts. He tells us (p. 178): "Public curiosity . . . attracted a large number of strangers to Rome, and a *bando* of the Pope, published two days before, *punished by death* anybody who did not respect the barrier. . . . On the 30th April, two hours before daylight, two masses were celebrated to implore the light of the Holy Spirit. Fontana, with all his staff, communicated. . . . On the eve of the lowering he had been blessed by the Holy Father. . . ." Before the work began Fontana told his workmen: "The work we are about to undertake is consecrated to religion, the exaltation of the Holy Cross"; thereon everyone recited with Fontana a *Pater* and an *Ave*. The ceremony was made interesting for the spectators by the presence of some "familiars" of the Church, whose duty it was to administer summary punishment to anyone who misbehaved. Absolute silence for workmen and spectators was ordered, and the story is still told of a workman who disregarded the order at a critical moment, when the ropes had become slack and could be tightened no further. He cried: "Wet the ropes!"—which was done, and the situation saved. For his initiative he is said to have had an annuity granted to himself and his descendants by the Pope.

The removal of the obelisk from Luxor Temple to the Place de la Concorde in Paris is perhaps the worst of these gross acts of vandalism, since the Luxor obelisks were the only pair still standing in their original position. It was done by an engineer called Lebas in 1836. The obelisk was lowered and raised by means of a huge compound sheers, consisting of five members, or struts, on each side of it. The power was supplied by systems of pulleys worked by capstans. The model shown in fig. 41 makes this method clear as regards the

FIG. 41. MODEL SHOWING HOW THE PARIS OBELISK WAS LOWERED AND ERECTED.
(*Page* 116.)

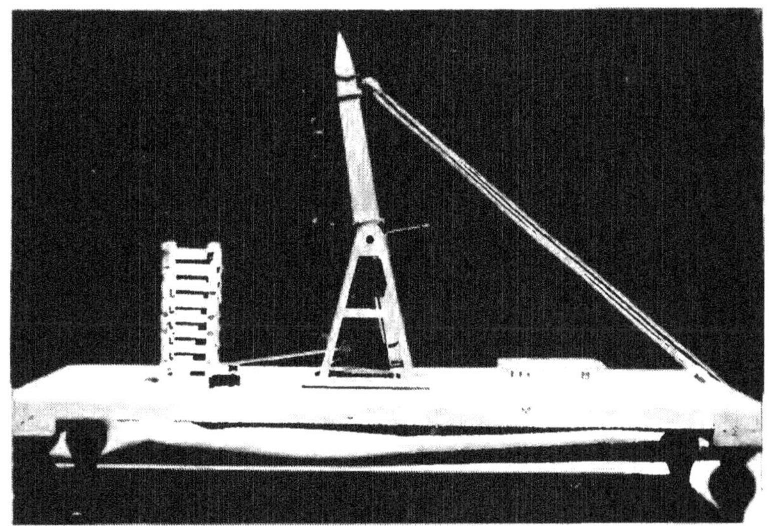

FIG. 42. MODEL TO SHOW HOW THE LOWERING AND THE RAISING OF THE NEW YORK OBELISK WERE PERFORMED.
(*Page* 117.)

appearance and position of the sheers, and the way in which the obelisk was slung from them, but only one capstan and system of pulleys is shown here. The obelisk was lowered on to a wooden cradle, on which it was dragged over a greased way, without rollers, to the Nile. There a pontoon-raft, with its prow temporarily removed, was waiting to receive it. The raft was towed home, the prow again removed and the obelisk dragged to the Place de la Concorde on its cradle, being finally brought up a slope leading up to the surface of the high pedestal on which it was to be erected. Though the obelisk weighed but 227 tons, it took a pull of 94 tons from the capstans to move it up the gradual incline. The edge of the obelisk was made to rest over the pedestal-notch, in which it engaged as it rose towards the vertical. Lebas's book, which is now very rare, is extremely interesting, giving many delightful sketches of some of the ludicrous situations met with in the course of the work, and of the cheery way in which the party overcame their difficulties, which ranged from an epidemic of plague to a shortage of wood.

The New York obelisk originally formed a pair with the London obelisk in a temple at Heliopolis, near Cairo, and both had been moved in Roman times to Alexandria, close to the beach (see p. 110). The English took the one which was lying in the sand, leaving the Americans the other, which was standing on its pedestal. At an earlier stage of its history all four edges had been broken away, and four copper cramps—shaped like sea-crabs—had been put at the corners to support it more firmly. In modern times only two of the crabs remained, the others having been stolen and blocks of stone put in their stead. The method of lowering the obelisk was ingenious in the extreme. The obelisk was first fitted with a pair of huge steel trunnions (similar to those seen on a toy cannon by means of which it can pivot around its centre). The trunnions were left loose until two steel towers had been constructed on either side of the obelisk, as shown in the model in fig. 42, to act as a support for them. A strong steel plate was passed under the butt of the obelisk and attached by a series of stout steel bars or " tension-rods," which could be shortened by screwing. Whether there was originally a space below the centre of the butt, or whether the obelisk was raised by jacks or rams placed under the four rounded-off corners, I am uncertain. (The plate and the tension-rods can best be seen in fig. 43.) The tension-rods were shortened by screwing, and the obelisk thus pulled clear off its pedestal, being supported by, and sliding through, the trunnion. The trunnion, which was arranged to be at the balancing-point of the obelisk when it was sufficiently high, was next bolted tight and the obelisk itself braced by long rods, passing, as shown in the model, over a stiff support at its centre. From this position it was intended to let the point of the obelisk come slowly round

Fig. 44. LOWERING OF THE NEW YORK OBELISK. TOWERS AND TRUNNIONS ABOUT TO BE REMOVED.
(Page 118.)

Fig. 44. LOWERING OF THE NEW YORK OBELISK. REMOVING THE WOODEN BAULKS FROM EACH END ALTERNATELY.
(Page 119.)

until it rested on a crib of wooden baulks (seen to the left in fig. 42). What actually happened was that, owing to a miscalculation of the balancing-point, the tip crashed down, breaking the holding-back ropes. It splintered about three courses of baulks and escaped breaking by a miracle. Another crib of baulks was next built below the butt, as shown in fig. 43. The next step was to remove the towers and the trunnions; this was done by taking the weight of the obelisk off them by raising the point by oil-rams placed within the wooden crib. For those unacquainted with rams, it may be explained that they are appliances by which a great lifting force can be obtained for a short distance by means of oil compressed into them by a pump. A "jack," which enables one man to lift up the back of a heavy motor, has a similar function. In the model shown, the jack is actuated by hand through a bowden wire. Fig. 43 shows the weight of the obelisk being taken by the ram, so that the towers and trunnions can be removed. This being done, the rams are released and the obelisk comes down on to the crib. The rams are then used from each crib in turn, lifting the tip or butt so that a course of baulks can be removed and the obelisk gently lowered on to the course below. Fig. 44 shows the obelisk when it has nearly arrived at the ground.

It had originally been intended to convey the obelisk through the streets of Alexandria to the harbour, but the inhabitants, especially the

European community, who had opposed the removal strenuously, influenced the Municipal Council to forbid this. A special wooden slide had therefore to be constructed so that the obelisk, which was to be put in a wooden caisson, could be pulled down it to the sea, and floated round to the harbour instead. At the harbour it was introduced into a steamship called the *Dessoug*, by opening a port in her bows. The journey to America was comparatively uneventful, and between the harbour and Central Park it did the longer journeys by rail and the shorter journeys rolling on cannon-balls running in U-shaped "channel-irons"; *i.e.*, cannon-balls were used as ball-bearings! At Central Park the erection was performed, with elaborate ceremonial, under the auspices of the Freemasons.

The method of erection was exactly the reverse of that used for the lowering, and it was carried out without a hitch on January 22, 1881, or just about 2½ years after the London obelisk was set up. The work done was under the direction of Lt.-Commander H. H. Gorringe, U.S. Navy.

Those who desire a complete account of al the removals of obelisks in mediæval and modern times cannot do better than consult Gorringe, *Egyptian Obelisks*, from which much of the information in this chapter has been taken. This book was published to celebrate the erection of the New York obelisk, and will form a most excellent textbook for future removals, in case it is decided to present the remaining Egyptian obelisks to Yugo-Slovakia, Liberia and the like. The question of transport is the book's real drawback, as its size almost demands a sled and rollers!

The London obelisk had only to be transported and erected, since it was already lying unbroken in the sand at Alexandria. The principle of the erecting process was the same as that used for the New York obelisk, except that, instead of the trunnions, steel shoulders with "knife-edge" bearing surfaces were used. These engaged in a huge wooden scaffolding instead of on the two steel towers. For transporting it by water it was enclosed in a steel shell, fitted, like a ship, with deck and mast. It even had watertight compartments. The "ship" was named the *Cleopatra*, and she set out from Egypt on the 21st of September, 1877. She steered very badly, and in a gale near Cape St. Vincent the steamship *Olga*, which was towing her home, had to cut the "august barge" adrift. Six sailors, who tried to reach the *Cleopatra* to secure her ballast, perished in the heavy sea. The *Olga* then lost the *Cleopatra*, and, imagining she had foundered, she steamed home. The *Cleopatra*, however, had not foundered at all, and was salved by a ship called the *Fitzmaurice*, who towed her into Ferrol. A claim for £5,000 salvage was reduced by the Admiralty Courts to £2,000. Having arrived in the Thames on January 20th, 1878, the obelisk was brought right up beside the site on the Thames Embankment where it now stands, being grounded at high tide. After the shell had been cut away, the lifting on to the Embankment was done almost entirely by hydraulic jacks.

At its erection, which took place in September, 1878, an extraordinary collection of objects was put in the base of this obelisk, which ranged from sets of coinage, newspapers and standard works, to a Mappin's shilling razor, *an Alexandra feeding-bottle,* a case of cigars and photographs of a dozen pretty Englishwomen for the benefit of posterity!

What would the feelings of Tuthmôsis III have been when he ordered these obelisks for the god Rê, had he known that one would be taken to a land of whose existence he never dreamed, and that the other would fall into the hands of what was then a savage people, and, after undergoing such vicissitudes as shipwreck and injuries from a German air-bomb, would still be standing, though thousands of miles away, after a lapse of nearly 3,500 years?

APPENDIX I

Dates of Egyptian Kings Mentioned in the Volume

Although the dates of the kings of the XVIIIth dynasty and onwards are known with great accuracy, there is a difference of opinion among scholars as to the dates of the kings between the Ist and the XIIth dynasties, which depends on whether the dark period between the XIIth and XVIIIth dynasties—which includes the Hyksos invaders—was long or short. Both the "long dating" and the "short dating" are given here.

XIth Dynasty

	L.D.	B.C.	S.D.
Menthuhotpe IV (?)	3592		2002

XIIth Dynasty (Complete)

	L.D.	B.C.	S.D.
(Amenemhêt I	2778		2000)
Senusret I	2758		1980
(Amenemhêt II	2716		1938)
(Senusret II	2684		1906)
(Senusret III	2660		1887)
Amenemhêt III..	2622		1849
(Amenemhêt IV	2758		1801)
(Sebeknefrurê	2569		1792)

XVIIIth Dynasty (Complete)

(Ahmôse I, "Amasis" I	1580–1557)
Amenophis I	1557–1501
Tuthmôsis I	
Tuthmôsis II	1501–1447
Tuthmôsis III and Hatshepsôwet ..	
Amenophis II..	1447–1420
Tuthmôsis IV..	1420–1411
Amenophis III	1411–1375
Amenophis IV, the heretic King Akhenaten	1375–1350
Sakerê	
Tutankhamûn	
Ay (Eye)	

XIXth Dynasty (Complete)

Haremhab	1350–1315
Ramesses I	1315–1314
Seti I	1313–1292
Ramesses II	1292–1225
(Merneptah	1225–1215)
(Amenmose	1215)
(Siptah	1215–1209)
Seti II	1209–1205

XXth Dynasty

Ramesses IV	1167–1161
Ramesses VI	1157–1142

XXVIth Dynasty

Psammetikhos II	593–588
Hophra	588–569
Amasis II	569–525

Ptolemaic

Ptolemy II, Philadelphus	286–247

APPENDIX II

Vocalisations of Egyptian Words.

The following variations in the transcription of ancient Egyptian and other names and words have been given to mitigate the sufferings of the general reader, who is appalled and annoyed by the great diversity of ways in which the ancient words are spelt, not only in the guide-books but in technical publications. As it has been noted in the preface, the method followed here has been to retain the Greek form if there are many variations and it seems passably close to the ancient pronunciation, otherwise to attempt to reconstruct its pronunciation in accordance with recent researches. This is the method used by the English philological school, as a supplement to the consonantal skeletons in use for all grammatical work throughout Europe and America.

The diacritical marks to show the different *h*'s, *s*'s, etc., have been omitted.

Key :—R.—Reconstructions.
G.—Greek forms.
X.—No data for vowels.
O.—Old style, which represents the ancient consonants and semi-vowels by *a*, *ȧ*, *ā*, *u*. If the word is still unpronounceable an *e* is added at any convenient place.

Those unmarked can mostly be proved incorrect.

'Ahmôse .. .. .. Amasis (G.); Amosis (G.); Aahmes.

'Ahmôse-pen-Nekhbeyet (R.) Ahmose - pen - nekhbet (R.); Aahmes-pen-nekhbet.

Amenemhêt (R.) .. .. Amenemmes (G.); Amenemhāt (O.).

Amenemôpet (R.) .. .. Amenemapt (O.); Amenappa (from cuneiform).

Amenôphis (G.) .. .. Amenothes (G.); Amenophthis (G.); Amenhotpe (R.); Amenhotep (R.); Amenhetep (O.).

Amen-Rê' (R.) .. .. Amunre (R.); Amen-Rā (O.); Ammon-Ra.

Amûn (R.) .. .. .. Amon (R.); Ammon (G.); Amen (O.); Amoun (Copt).

(This becomes " Amen- " when unaccented.)

Aswân (modern use) .. Syene (G.); Assouan (Fr.); Asswan.

Aten (X.) .. .. .. Aton (X.); Adon (X.).

Beknekhonsu (R.) .. .. Bakenkhonsu (O.); Bekenkhensu (O.).

Dhuthotpe (R.) .. .. Dhuthotep (R.); Thuthotep (R.); Tehutihetep (O.).

[1]Dhutiy (R.).. .. .. Thutiy (R.); Tehuty (O.); Tahuti, &c.

Haremhab (R.) .. .. Harmhab (R.); Haremheb (R.); Harmhabi (R.); Horemheb; (H)armais (G.).

Hatshepsôwet (R.) .. Hatshepsuit (R.); Hatshepsut (O.); Hatshepsu, Hatshopsitu, Chnemtamon, Hatasoo.

Hepusonb (R.) .. .. Hapusenb (O.); Hepuseneb (R.).

Ineni (R.X.) .. .. Anena (O.X.); Anna.

Khepri (X.) .. .. Khepera (O.); Khepra (O.), and others.

Makerê' (R.) .. .. Maāt-ka-Rā (O.); Ra-Maāt-Ka.

Menkheperra'-sonb (R.) .. Menkheperraseneb (R.).

Menmirê' (R.) .. .. Men-Maāt-Ra (O.); Rā-Maāt-Men; Rā-men-Maāt.

Menthuhotpe (R.) .. .. Menthuhotep (R.); Mentuhetep (O.); Menthuhetep (O.).

[1] It is quite likely that the D was pronounced T in the New Kingdom, but the D is the more usually used transliteration.

Monthu (R.)	Menthu (O.); (Her)month(is) (G.); (Er)-mont (Copt); (Ar)-mant (Arab).
Nefrurê' (R.)..	Neferu-Rā (O.).
'Okheperkerê' (R.)	Aa-Kheper-Ka-Rā; Rā-Āa-Kheper-Ka.
Psammetikhos (G.) ..	Psamthek (R.); Psamtek (O.); &c.
Ra'- (unaccented)	Rā.
Ramesses (G.)	Rāmses (R.); Rāmessu (O.); Rameses (O.); Rhamsesis (G.); Ramsasa, &c.
Ra'môse (R.)	Rāmes (O.).
Rekhmirê' (R.)	Rakhmirê (R.); Rekhmarā (O.).
Rê' (in accented syllables)	Rā (O.); Rē (Copt).
Sennemût (R.)	Senemût (R.); Senmût (O.).
Seti (O.)	Sethos (G).; Sethoy (R.); Sety (O.).
Tut'ankhamûn (R.) ..	Tutenkhamon (R.); Tutankh-amen (O.), and many other versions, some frivolous.
Tuthmôsis (G.)	Thutmose (R.); Dhutmose (R.); Tahutimes; Thothmes; Thutmosis.

INDEX

(For various methods of transcribing Egyptian names, see Appendix II)

Printed in Great Britain by Hazell, Watson & Viney, Ld., London and Aylesbury.